Getting Started with Demand Generation

Developing an All-Star Marketing Strategy to Supercharge Growth and Minimize Risk

Matt Berringer, MBA

First Edition

ISBN: 9781793986801

Contents

13 chpter

Introduction

My goal with this book is to give you the knowledge and tools to develop a high-performing demand generation program that delivers quality, sales-ready opportunities to your sales team.

This strategy is based on more than 15 years of experience in various marketing and communication roles, in companies with as few as two employees and as many as thousands, in startups and well-established firms.

With each position I learned something about the role that marketing plays in demand generation. This book lays out those lessons.

One of the biggest takeaways is that there are no silver bullets. The marketing industry and just about every other industry is overrun with quick fix solutions, hacks, and Holy Grail-type solutions. I wish I could tell you that demand generation was something that could easily be hacked. But the truth is that demand generation is not simple; it takes a lot of work to get a program running and even more to make sure it's running well.

Another takeaway is that marketing (and demand generation) is a company-wide initiative. Everybody is a part of the marketing team. And the marketing team is part of every other team as well. The days of siloed departments fighting turf wars and passing blame are over. There is too much competition, and customers are way too used to world-class experiences to put up with being underserved. For your demand generation program to succeed, teamwork is essential and alignment is critical.

We'll get into teamwork in a bit, but this book is called *Getting Started with Demand Generation,* so first let's take a step back and think about what that means.

What is demand generation?

Despite its increasing popularity, demand generation is defined differently depending on whom you ask. Here is how the bastion of all truth, Wikipedia, defines it:

> *Demand generation is the focus of targeted marketing programs to drive awareness and interest in a company's products and/or services. Commonly used in business-to-business, business-to-government, or longer business-to-consumer sales cycles, demand generation involves multiple areas of marketing and is really the marriage of marketing programs coupled with a structured sales process.*

While Wikipedia's information can sometimes be suspect, this definition is fairly accurate. But if I had to put it more simply, I'd say demand generation is a strategically planned, persona-focused marketing program. While brochures, collateral, and logos are important parts of a company's foundation, demand generation marketing is focused on orchestrated campaigns that support the buyer throughout the buying process and (as a result) drive qualified opportunities to the sales team.

Without question, brand is important. In fact there's an argument to be made for its increasing importance. The problem arises when we use *branding* as a way to hide from accountability. If you or people on your team would rather hide behind refreshing a brochure that probably doesn't need it or creating more collateral to gather dust in a storage room instead of figuring out how you can better support your prospects, demand generation might not be for you.

If, however, you like the idea of thoughtfully putting together campaigns built on persona-based insights, launching them, driving real business impact, analyzing the results, and improving from there, welcome aboard!

It might sound risky to make this transition and, to be fair, it is a big change from marketing's traditional role. But the real risk is in not adapting to a changing marketplace and becoming a relic of the past.

Demand generation is a TEAM sport

As someone who has been a member of high performing teams and those who have been sabotaged by political, me-first attitudes, I know it's important to define the difference between a *team* and a *TEAM*. A *team* is people of varying skill levels thrown together in the department stew. Some are hired by the department manager and some were probably inherited from another manager. Their motivations are varied as is their commitment.

Ego often takes precedence over team accomplishments, and that often leads to an activity > results mentality. Team members are more interested in showing the volume of work they (alone) have completed as compared to their co-workers (not teammates).

At one time or another we've all been a part of these types of teams. Ironically, these are often the departments where people throw around the word *team* more than any other, as if saying it more will make the team function as one…

The good news is that we can (and have to) change the atmosphere of these departments, and we'll do that by building a shared vocabulary, developing common goals, and sharing accountability.

In contrast to a team in name only, a *TEAM* is a collaborative group of people with common interests, shared language, and common expectations. With this group, ego takes a backseat to getting the job done and results are valued over activity volume.

One other note on this concept: in the traditional sense, all-star team is built around high performers at each position. It is not based on one highly skilled person doing all the work or telling others what to do. For this (and frankly any program) to work, your team and other departments need to unite under a common purpose. That purpose? Helping prospects and customers achieve their goals in an efficient, enlightened, and effective manner. Our goal is to make them feel as though a team of all-stars has been developed specifically to help them get the job done. There are too many other companies doing this well for customers to settle for anything less.

Why all-star?

Another big lesson I've learned over the years is that there are no right or wrong answers in marketing. As I mentioned earlier, there are no sliver bullets. Put the work into preparation and planning and take your best shot. Then perform an unfiltered, dispassionate assessment of what was done, how it was done, what worked, and what didn't. Do more of what worked, less of what didn't, and try something new next time. This creates a cycle of constant improvement that virtually guarantees your results are going to improve.

This process is similar to the selection process for all-star games. Players are selected based on their performance. That's what we're aiming to do in building and optimizing our demand generation program. We're going to plan our strategy, put our pieces in play, record performance, and continually improve based on the results.

There are many people out there would would like to have us believe that there is only one way to do marketing. Some say inbound marketing is the only thing that matters. Others say outbound sales is the only reliable way to drive results. More recently account-based marketing has been hailed as the golden child.

Why choose? We don't have to align ourselves with one dogma and live or die with it no matter what. Instead, we're going to take a lesson from martial arts legend Bruce Lee:

Unfortunately, most students in the martial arts are conformists. Instead of learning to depend on themselves for expression, they blindly follow their instructors, no longer feeling alone, and finding security in mass imitation. The product of this imitation is a dependent mind. Independent inquiry, which is essential to genuine understanding, is sacrificed.

Look around the martial arts and witness the assortment of routine performers, trick artists, desensitized robots, glorifiers of the past and so on — all followers or exponents of organized despair.

- Bruce Lee

As marketers, we don't want to fall into the same trap. We're supposed to be the fun, artsy, creative weirdos, right? So why on earth would we align to one methodology? That's not fun, artsy, creative, or effective.

Click-baity articles that claim one tactic or another is dead might generate traffic for the author, but they don't generate a holistic, personalized, results-focused strategy. So instead of chasing after squirrels like the dog in *Up*, we're going to build a program that takes a scientific approach; testing, measuring, and responding based on real results.

Not aligning to one camp or the other allows us to maximize our results and minimize our risk. Proclaiming that inbound marketing is the best and doggedly refusing to engage in any outbound marketing exposes us to risk. Saying that sales is more important than marketing or that customer support doesn't have a role, kicks players off the team before we even start the game. Instead, we want to pack the clubhouse with every skill and asset we can so that we can bring each to bear against the challenges we face on the field. This maximizes our chances for success and builds a collaborative, empowered, team-first atmosphere that drives results, not meaningless activity.

Always look for the best of the best, do more of what works and get rid of what doesn't.

Are you ready for demand generation?

Before you jump into building a demand generation program, there's one very important thing to consider. Have you *really* figured out product-market fit? Is your product *really* ready for the market? This might sound easy, but it is one of the toughest questions to answer, especially for startups.

After all, we believe in the solution we're offering and we see the value. If we see the value, then the market will as well, right? Not so fast. In fact, according to a recent study by Startup Genome, 70 percent of startups scaled prematurely along some dimension and startups typically needed two to three times longer to validate the market than the owners expected.

Don't get fooled into thinking you need to scale and build out your sales and marketing teams at an exponential rate based on what could be flawed early data (early adopters willing to try anything vs. mass market readiness).

If you're wrong, and you scale your team too quickly, your payroll skyrockets while revenue stagnates. This disconnect puts even more pressure on your team to deliver revenue before the market has validated your solution. That can lead to poor customer experiences, bad word of mouth, and running out of cash. It can also lead to a situation where you don't know whether the demand generation program is failing or it's something else. In this scenario, you could have an industry-leading demand generation program that does everything right but still fails to deliver results because the product is not resonating with the market.

So how do you know when you're ready? Venture capitalist Marc Andreessen talks about product-market fit as a feeling rather than a binary event. He says that when you don't have the right fit, sales cycles are slow and fall apart, word-of-mouth doesn't happen organically, and the feedback you're getting isn't overwhelmingly positive. When you do have proper fit, people are finding you faster than you can make the product, sales cycles are short, reviews are off the charts, customers are renewing like crazy, etc.

I suggest you approach product-market fit just like a lot of the other practices outlined in this book: take the time to get the basics right before complicating things. Crawl before you walk. Walk before you run. Preparing and focusing on the fundamentals now will help you move much faster when the time is right.

A quick note on how the book is organized

I've organized this book in the way that I would approach developing a program from the ground up. The discussion becomes detailed very quickly, so feel free to jump around if you aren't ready for the heavy stuff right now. For the most part, the chapters can be digested independently. Also, if you're brand new to demand generation and marketing there might be some alphabet soup or terms that don't make sense. Skip to Chapter 12 before you start to get brief definitions for some commonly used words and acronyms.

One last thing: I'll be posting related worksheets and templates on my website. Download them at demandgenconsulting.com.

By applying the process outlined in this book, you're going to develop an efficient and effective all-star demand generation program that supercharges growth, minimizes risk, and keeps evolving to meet your goals. Ready to get started? Let's go!

Chapter 1

Developing a

Common Language

The single biggest problem in communication is the
illusion that it has taken place.

George Bernard Shaw

Why it's so important to develop
a common language

This is a book about demand generation, so why start with language? It's all
about alignment. If you don't have a crystal clear vision and common
understandings within and across teams, you're doomed from the start.

A lack of common understanding takes us down the lowercase *team* path.
People develop their own ideas of what is important, which invariably differ
from what others think, and just like that, you're on your way to
dysfunction, misunderstanding, and unmet expectations before your first
campaign is underway. Think about the common language as the rules to
the game. If you have a different idea of the rules than your teammates do,

you're bound to run into misunderstandings. But if everyone is reading from the same rulebook and playing by those rules, you're much less likely to run into complications. Later, if there are disagreements, you can go back to the rule book to remedy the problem.

Also, when we say *language*, we're talking about basic things like terms (prospect, lead, opportunity, etc.) but we're also talking about process and goals.

In order to develop this common understanding, many organizations recommend developing a service level agreement between marketing and sales. In general, these agreements are between a vendor and a customer, and they outline the level of service the customer can expect from the supplier. That way if there are any disagreements about the level of service, both parties can refer back to this agreement and use it to help resolve the issue.

While this practice is generally used for external vendor to customer agreements, we can also use it for our internal customers. By defining and mutually agreeing on the terms of the service between departments, the majority of misunderstandings and "Who's on first?" moments can be avoided.

Developing a service level agreement

What goes into a service level agreement? For me, this is the perfect place to define common terms, processes, and of course, metric-based goals. This is also where I would lay out the path we want a prospect to take as we develop them into a qualified opportunity, which means we'll lay out the marketing funnel here as well.

At a minimum this agreement should include:

- Quantitative Goals
    - Opportunities
    - Leads
    - Prospects
    - Revenue Generated
    - Pipeline Generated
    - Campaign Activities (Trade Shows, Outbound, Content Development)
- Defining Common Terms and Criteria
    - The Marketing Funnel
        - Lead Stages (Open, Lead, Qualifying, MQL, SQL)
    - The Sales Funnel
        - Opportunity Stages
- Common Processes
    - How qualified opportunities are handed off to account executives
    - Reporting Expectations
    - Workflows

responsibility
Who does what

Quantitative goals

One of the biggest sources of tension between marketing and sales can be avoided if we take goal-setting seriously. Typically, sales teams become upset because either the quantity or the quality of those leads is not what they expected. Working together to define your quantitative goals in this section and the criteria for these goals in the next section can go a long way towards aligning those expectations across departments. This will help promote collaboration, empathy, and alignment across the teams. If the marketing team doesn't get buy-in from the sales team, you're on the path to dysfunction. If they think your goals are too low, even if you hit your numbers, they aren't going to be happy.

In order to develop marketing goals that the sales team is on board with, executive leadership will first work together with sales and marketing to determine overall revenue goals and expected contributions from each department. In other words, if our revenue goal is one million dollars, how much of that should be sourced directly by our sales team, and how much should come from marketing, sales development, and customer success (renewals, up-sells, etc.)?

How do you decide on numbers that are fair? It depends on the existing capabilities of your department, the strength of your product, growth in the industry, growth of competitors, and more. Check out the Sales Benchmark Index (salesbenchmarkindex.com) for more information. They have done an amazing job of thinking through the process and provide a lot of research that can help build your model.

With a revenue target and a contribution percentage developed for the year, we work backwards from that number to define how many opportunities, leads, prospects, and contacts marketing will need to generate in order to achieve that goal. This is where accurate data from your customer relationship management (CRM) software can really drive accurate predictions because you can predict how may leads will be needed based on your conversion rates.

Here are some example conversion rate benchmarks. These numbers will vary by channel and by industry. See Chapter 12 for definitions of the acronyms.

Prospect to Lead conversion rate: 10 percent

Lead to MQL: 25 percent

MQL to SQL: 75 percent

Opportunity Win rate: 25 percent

If you don't have it, this is also the right time to note what data you would need to make these decisions and to begin collecting it in a formal manner.

Here's a quick example of what quantitative goals could look like for a one million dollar pipeline target using the conversion rates above and and average deal value of $100K. We're going to work backwards from the target revenue goal.

1. If we need one million in revenue, and our win rate is at 25 percent, we need to generate four times that much ($4M) in pipeline to assure we hit that one million mark.
2. If each deal is roughly $100K, we're going to need ten closed-won deals to hit our revenue target, but we know that we need to generate 4x that number because of the 25 percent win rate. So we need 10 x 4 (40 opportunities) to hit our goal.
3. If we need 40 opportunities, and 75 percent of our MQLs convert to opportunities, how many MQLs do we need? For that, we just take 40 and divide it by 75 percent to get approximately 54 MQLs.
4. Stay awake - we're almost there!
5. To get the number of leads we need, we just take 54 and divide that by the 25 percent conversion rate to calculate a goal of 216 leads.
6. And finally, in order to generate enough prospects to get this whole train moving, we divide that 216 leads number by the 10 percent conversion rate. And we get 2160.

7. That's about as far as we can go with a general example but now that you have your hard numbers, you can dive in and begin dividing it down by months and weeks to set SMART (we'll define SMART in the next section) goals for each. You'll also want to take into account any seasonality which may occur in your industry.

8. With these numbers in place, you can then set out to determine which channel is going to contribute which percentage of prospects and leads. This flows directly into the strategy piece of the program which we'll discuss in the next chapter. These two elements will need to be developed simultaneously; your goals will be broken down into a strategy and tactics for achieving them.

A quick note on goal-setting

The greater danger for most of us lies not in setting our aim too high and falling short;
but in setting our aim too low, and achieving our mark.

- Michelangelo

It can be very tempting to set a low bar in an attempt to make you and your team look like rock stars. Don't fall into that trap. Proper goals should make you feel a little nervous. The goals you set should not be slam dunks, and they should not be so outlandish that there's no way you or anyone could ever achieve them. I'm a big proponent of the SMART goals framework. Make each goal Specific, Measurable, Achievable, Realistic, and Time-Bound. And then break them down into even smaller monthly, weekly, and even daily chunks to keep your team on track. *— Quarterly Holiday, etc.*

The way you approach goal-setting and goal measurement goes a long way toward how your team will perform over the long haul. It's important to make your team feel comfortable in setting stretch goals and in building an environment that makes it OK to fail, to learn why the goal wasn't met, and to adjust for next time. Setting the bar too low not only hurts your revenue impact but also sets the stage for complacency and boredom. In fact, there are some organizations which penalize employees for always achieving their goals. The idea is that if the goal is always being achieved, it is not challenging enough.

Defining common terms

On a recent trip to Japan, my wife (who lived there for two years and speaks a decent amount of the language) informed me that she was having a hard time with the difference between the Japanese word for hospital (*byōin*) and the one for beauty salon (*biyōin*). Big difference! I could just picture her standing there after I injured myself doing something stupid, telling locals that she needed to get me to a hairdresser right away…

Take the time now to make sure that your teams are communicating clearly so that there's no miscommunication and each knows what the other means when it counts!

One quick note here: it's important that everyone in your company knows the difference between the marketing funnel and the sales funnel. Don't be afraid to go back to basics and make sure that everyone is on the same page. Often terms like *funnel* and *pipeline* are thrown around, and we forget that people may have a different idea of what that means.

In my experience these marketing and sales funnels are often conflated, which can lead to misunderstandings. You will have to define the funnels as you see fit. Some companies may want to have a giant marketing and sales funnel. However, because the departments have different core

22

responsibilities (marketing generally focuses on qualified opportunities, sales generally focuses on closed deals), I prefer to have different funnels for each, one that feeds into the other. There is (and should be) overlap as well, marketing will play a part in helping close sales and sales will play a role in developing new business.

For this model, the marketing funnel is everything that leads up to a qualified opportunity being passed to an account executive.

Sample Marketing Funnel and Definitions

Prospect Contact has not engaged directly but is on our radar. (Website visitor, trade show attendee, employee at target company, member of target persona professional organization)
Open Lead Prospect has taken some action to engage with the company. Action needs to be taken to qualify them. (Website download, webinar attendee, mailing list sign up)
Working Lead Our team is actively trying to contact the lead.
Qualifying Lead Lead has been contacted by a member of our team and has responded positively but has not been fully qualified yet.
Marketing Qualified Lead - MQL - Opportunity Lead has been contacted by a member of our team and has been declared as qualified by meeting the baseline criteria for an opportunity. An opportunity is created by the person who conducted the qualifying conversation (most likely an SDR). The SDR sets up a hand-off meeting to introduce the contact and the AE.
Sales Qualified Lead - SQL - Opportunity The hand-off meeting has been conducted. The AE and SDR have debriefed and agreed that the opportunity is valid. The AE will pursue it from here.

*Note: I've found that my definition for MQL is a bit different from that of some organizations. Many might put the Qualifying Leads into the MQL bucket. I like keeping the bar for MQLs high. This establishes a level of quality that otherwise can become pretty muddied by throwing every Qualifying Lead in there. Again, you'll have to figure out what works for your organization and your goals. You'll also note that there is some intentional overlap here between an SQL and an Opportunity. This drives home the handoff between marketing and sales.

Is the funnel dead?

Lately, some organizations have been trying to push people away from the traditional funnel model and encouraging them to think more about the entire prospect-to-customer-to-evangelist lifecycle as a flywheel. This holistic view is an important concept that I discuss more in chapter eight. I encourage you to think about the nomenclature as you develop your program and find what works best for your team, but don't get too hung up on change for change's sake. Too many superficial changes can demotivate your team and leave them wondering if there really is an overarching strategy that brings it all together or if you are just hopping from one trend to the next without any follow-through. Call it a funnel, call it a flywheel, invert the funnel and call it a pyramid, just make sure everyone knows what you mean.

When is someone qualified?

This is an important conversation that needs to happen between sales and marketing and one that should be as objectively defined as possible. Leaving this to be subjectively decided can lead to trouble, so developing some sort of scoring system is an effective way to make sure everyone is on the same page.

One method that has been around forever and many people still use is the BANT (Budget, Authority, Need, Timeline) qualification framework. Essentially, companies use those four criteria to decide whether a prospect is ready to make a purchase. Do they have a budget defined? Do they have the authority to make the purchase? Do they have a specific need defined? And do they have a timeline in which they want to make a purchase?

You can get more complicated, but I've found BANT to be an effective and simple way to quickly qualify/disqualify prospects. You will just need to come to agreement around how many of the BANT criteria need to be met for a lead to be qualified.

For example, if a lead meets 50 percent of the criteria (they have the budget and the authority to purchase), the rep can move it to qualified. This is a quick and dirty way to do it, but it's a good way to get started. The more complex the qualification process is, the easier it is to get confused. Start simple and look for ways to improve. You can always refine it as you go.

Another useful tool for qualifying/disqualifying prospects is a lead scorecard. Using this tool and working from an ideal customer profile, we can set up a rubric for the qualifying conversation. The questions can mirror the BANT qualification or get more detailed. The qualifying rep asks several questions and puts a 1 or 0 after each question.

If the total passes our threshold, we pass it on. If not, it goes to the lead nurturing workflow. Below is a quick idea of what this can look like. You would insert a one in for each *Yes* answer and a zero for each *No*:

Name:

Title: Company:

Email:

Does title match a key persona?	1
Is there a defined need for what we offer?	1
Is prospect using a competitor product?	0
Is the size of the company greater than X?	0
Total	2

If the total is two or greater, the lead is qualified and ready for sales follow up. If not, it gets put into a separate workflow for follow up by the marketing team.

Sample sales funnel and definitions

Sales Stage	Exit Criteria
Marketing qualified lead	Positive customer response to presentation
Sales qualified lead	Budget, timing, and authority clarified
Discovery	Customer needs are addressable
Solution identified	Customer agrees to success metrics
Demo/Evaluation	Customer selects your solution
Negotiation	Customer agrees to business and legal terms
Closed	All required documents received

Common processes

When defining common processes, you have a chance to decide how things happen in, and between, the marketing and sales departments. Some common processes to cover here include:

- How qualified opportunities are handed off to account executives
- Reporting expectations
- Workflows

Handing off qualified opportunities

This one is first because getting qualified opportunities from the marketing team to account executives is important. Your marketing team has worked so hard to develop leads into opportunities, so let's make sure none of them fall through the cracks because one team thinks the other is following up.

The best way to ensure a smooth hand-off is to require a live transition. This is where the person who has qualified the lead schedules a meeting with the lead, the account executive, and her/himself. This makes sure that everyone is on the same page and lets your SDRs and AEs develop a closer working relationship. Of course, this isn't always possible and in those cases, I recommend that the SDR or marketing team secure some sort of written confirmation that the AE is taking charge of the opportunity.

Reporting expectations

When determining the language that surrounds reporting expectations, consider which reports will be generated, by whom, how often they will be distributed, and to whom.

Workflows

Here you can outline what the desired workflows for activities look like. This can include things like campaign requests, trade show requests, lead processing expectations (how quickly will something be turned around?), and anything else you feel sales and marketing should have in common knowledge.

Wrapping up

In closing, there is a reason I put the common language part at the front of this book. It is imperative to your team and your company that each department (not just sales and marketing) operates under a common vision and expectations. When you do the dirty work first, you create a foundation for success and make it so much easier for your teams to work together towards a common purpose rather than arguing over who should do what. Put the work in now; you won't regret it!

Chapter 2

Defining Your Demand

Generation Strategy

Sound strategy starts with having the right goal.

Michael Porter, Harvard Business School

Now that we've laid out what we want to achieve and we have a common language for talking about what we're doing, it's time to think about just what and how we're going to do it. There are a number of ways to think about demand generation, and over the years a lot of people seem to want to make us pick sides.

They sound something like this:

• "Only inbound works these days."

- "People don't answer the phone anymore. You need to make them come to you."
- "Inbound is lazy. You need to be hitting the phones every single day, before work, after work, and on the weekends."
- "Outbound is the only true way to drive predictable results."

So who is right?

First, let's take a step back and examine inbound and outbound to see each can bring to the table.

Looking inbound

What's the big idea?

Thanks to the internet, the buying process for many B2B and B2C goods and services has changed significantly over the past 20 years. With a wealth of information just a click away, buyers are much more likely to do their own research rather than reach out directly to a salesperson or wait for a salesperson to call.

Inbound is a response to that. The idea is that because consumers are doing their own research, and not reaching out to companies until much later in the buying process, companies need to find a new way to establish a relationship with consumers.

Enter inbound. Resources like ebooks, webinars, and videos help companies build relationships for the long term. The hypothesis is that if the consumer sees your company as an advocate and a thought leader before they need help, they are much more likely to turn to you when they actually need help.

Examples of inbound resources:

- eBooks
- Worksheets
- Checklists
- Infographics
- Webinars
- Blogs
- Videos
- Slack channels
- Messaging apps
- Podcasts, Webcasts, Facebook Live
- Landing pages and website pages optimized for keyword searches
- Sponsored content
- In-person inbound
    - Exclusive dinners
    - Open user groups
    - Free classes

Inbound positives

Inbound presents a ton of benefits that can help your company build a long-term relationship with potential customers and existing customers.

Leads are more engaged in your communications - If you've ever seen email stats of an opt-in email vs. a cold email, you've seen the power of opt-in lists. Engagement rates like opens and clicks can be 5x higher with opt-in lists.

In my experience opt-in emails typically hit *at least* a 20 percent open rate and cold emails can range anywhere from the low single-digit percents (or, eek... zero) up to 15-20 if you're lucky.

Leads are more willing to engage - A few years ago my wife had an issue with the bumper on her car. A rivet came loose and it began scraping on the ground. She took it to a repair shop and was cringing while she waited to see how much it was going to cost. Fifteen minutes later, the mechanic popped out of the garage and handed her the car keys. "No charge. Come back when you have a real problem," he said. He fixed the car and built trust with her. Guess who she called the next time she needed help?

If I were you, I'd need more than an anecdote to convince me. Here's some data from the Rain Group on how talented salespeople get the job done:

So we studied more than 700 buyers representing $3.1 billion in annual B2B purchases across multiple industries to learn what sales winners did differently from sellers who came in second.

We found that sales winners consistently do three things: They connect, convince, and collaborate with buyers. Our research found that sales winners make strong personal connections at more than double the rate of second-place finishers (Schultz).

For sales and marketing teams to be successful, building trust and relationships early is critical.

The process is buyer-driven - Prospects choose when to interact and what to interact with based on their needs. Because the resources are mapped to the stages of the buyer's journey (we'll get to this later), we can figure out where they are in the buying process. You aren't guessing based on five minutes of research on LinkedIn or blindly calling contacts on a purchased list.

The data is from the source - Data quality is invaluable no matter which marketing strategy you employ. By having the buyer input the data, you are getting the info straight from the source. This means there are fewer worries about dirty and outdated data. Of course, you will also run into the Bart Simpsons of the world who won't enter the right data. They are generally pretty easy to spot, and you can build in automatic workflows to weed them out.

It can raise your company's profile - By choosing the right content partners, thought leaders, and publishers, you can effectively piggy-back on the trust they've built with their audience.

Your company will better understand your target audience's needs and challenges - Part of the process of developing inbound resources is studying your target audience and understanding what makes them tick. This can be extremely beneficial when you are engaging with them in person or on the phone.

Happier sales people - Ask any account executive whether they'd rather have a lead that has reached out directly to the company or a cold prospect, and you'll understand why inbound makes for happy sales people.

It's scaleable - This is huge. Inbound resources are always on. They are not limited to the amount of outreach your staff can physically perform or the talent of the people performing that outreach. Once developed, persona-centered resources can continue to generate leads for months and even years after they are published.

Inbound negatives

It takes a long time - This is a big one and one you need to make everyone aware of when working on inbound. Before even getting started, we need to create personas which will help guide our resource development. This takes time on its own. Then we need time to develop the actual resources. THEN, we need to develop resources that will nurture the buyer through the journey and eventually qualify them as a sales-ready opportunity. Depending on the industry and the product you are selling, it can take days, months, and even years to get from the top of the funnel to the bottom.

Driving traffic can be a challenge - OK, so you've worked really hard on developing your persona, you've then created an awesome resource based on that persona, you publish the landing page and then...crickets. There are things we can do to avoid this, but you need to be prepared with a promotional strategy that will drive quality traffic. That said, inbound performance can be a bit unpredictable.

Attribution can be tough - If someone engages with a piece of content and then falls silent for several months and a salesperson meets them at a trade show, should the marketing team get any credit for that initial engagement? You'll want to figure out how to attribute leads that cross multiple channels.

It's an investment - In order to set up the plumbing to attract, convert, and nurture leads without going insane, you'll probably want to invest in a platform to help manage the resources and provide analytics. This takes money, and you'll also need someone to configure and manage it.

It is difficult to target a specific company - If you have target accounts, it can be tough to specifically target them with a purely inbound approach because the process is buyer-driven.

There are a lot of ways mess it up - Ask anybody who has engaged with inbound in the past ten years, and I'm willing to bet they will have a story to tell about something that didn't work. There are a lot of ways to fail at inbound; here are a few to avoid:

- Creating content that is company-centric, not buyer-centric
- Not creating enough content to properly nurture leads into qualified opportunities
- Not creating persona-specific content
- Not segmenting and following up with relevant content based on engagement
- Following up too soon
- Not following up in a timely manner with people who've asked for more information

Looking outbound

What's the big idea?

At the risk of sounding ancient, the internet has drastically impacted just about every aspect of our lives. The buying process has changed, but as we noted earlier, inbound can take a considerable amount of time to execute.

Not everyone has the time it takes to build and implement a fully functional inbound process.

The idea behind outbound is that by providing personalized, timely, 1:1 outreach, companies can outperform automated marketing, expand brand awareness, find low hanging fruit, begin building relationships, and more predictably build pipeline. I also include mass marketing and trade shows in the outbound bucket. Because trade shows are a large part of outbound marketing and have unique traits, I've separated their pros and cons into sub-sections.

Examples of outbound tactics and resources

- Phone calls
- Drop-ins
- 1:1 emails
- Mass emails to non-subscribers or purchased lists
- Social media engagement
- Advertising (Digital and Traditional)
- Trade shows
- Direct mail

Outbound positives

Shorter time to qualified opportunity - This is one of the reasons outbound is still so popular among many companies. Rather than building a system that essentially engineers demand (inbound), we're going out and finding demand that already exists. That means that typically there is a shorter time from identifying a lead to converting it to an opportunity.

More direct measurement - As a I mentioned earlier, inbound can be a little tricky to measure. You can do it, but outbound is certainly a much more linear measurement. (e.g., We reached out to this many contacts, performed this many activities, got this many meetings, which turned into this many opportunities.) Combine that internal data with external benchmarks and you can quickly identify areas for improvement.

One of the toughest things to track down can be benchmarks, so I put a section at the end of the book that shares the ones that I've used along with their sources.

It puts a personal face on your brand - When done right (and many times it isn't!), outbound can be an extension of your public relations strategy. Conducting personalized, empathetic outreach reminds people that there is a human on the other end. If your team members are interacting with contacts in a way that leaves them with a positive impression, even if they don't end up buying, they're much more likely to remember you at the next trade show or the next time their current vendor screws up.

It's more focused - Unlike inbound, outbound makes targeting specific regions, companies, or people a no-brainer. So if there are companies you know would be the right fit, you don't have to wait for them to come to you - you can reach out and start building that relationship right away.

It's more accurate - When you talk to someone at a target account, the information you receive is direct from the source. You're not relying on what you can glean from an old press release or a Twitter feed which hasn't been updated in years. Again, even if the account is not ready to buy now, you can use the intelligence you gather for future conversations or to zero in on when you reach out again.

Trade show positives

They are still effective - One of my favorite radio shows hosts singles mixers throughout the year. For weeks leading up to the mixer, they take calls from single people and add them to the guest list. Without fail, the day following the mixer is filled with calls from people who met someone and had an amazing time.

This illustrates why trade shows still work. Just like the singles at the mixer, people at trade shows are already pre-screened. They know what they want, and many come with a list of vendors to visit. The key is doing your homework and making sure the people who are attending the show fit your ideal persona and customer profile. Here are some other reasons trade shows should be a part of your outbound strategy.

Attendees are already out of their comfort zone - For most people, a day on the job doesn't involve sitting in rooms full of strangers, listening to big names speak, and eating out for every meal. Because attendees are already out of their normal comfort zone, you may be able to inspire them to think differently and interact in ways that they wouldn't if they were behind their desk.

They know they are going to interact with vendors - Running into vendors on the show floor, at a happy hour or elsewhere is expected if you're an attendee. You aren't interrupting them in the way that a cold call or cold email does.

Simply being there can raise the company's profile - Sales and marketing leaders have this discussion year in and year out. Is it worth going? The account executives argue that even though last year's show results weren't the best in terms of leads, the company *has* to be there just to be taken seriously. While demand generation focuses primarily on the tactics that drive tangible results, it is important to consider brand development and awareness as part of your strategy.

Outbound negatives

It only works when your reps do - Unlike the 24-7, always-on nature of inbound, outbound only works when your reps are pushing the buttons. That means your target market can be limited by budgeting/staffing limitations.

People really are ducking calls more - Recent research from Jive Communications shows that 77 percent of respondents admit they duck sales calls. But don't worry, sales folks aren't alone: 22 percent of respondents said they don't answer calls from their supervisors, and 20 percent admitted to ignoring their calls from their mothers at times.

It can be intrusive - Outbound can be a delicate balance between being persistent and being annoying, and the trouble is that balance can be different for each contact you're attempting to reach. We'll discuss how to avoid being annoying in the following chapters.

It can be tough on reps - As my awkward, teenage self could have told you, dealing with rejection on a daily basis can be taxing and demoralizing. The Bridge Group estimates the average tenure for an SDR is around 6-12 months (18 months max). For outbound to be successful you'll need to build a strong culture that's relentlessly positive, supportive, and provides regular training for improving performance.

It only works when your reps do (redux) - As mentioned above, outbound can work only when your reps are working. It also works only when they are performing (working) well. Performance can vary drastically based on the rep. In contrast, inbound performance is much less volatile.

There are no magic bullets - While personas typically have similar challenges and goals, personalities are of course going to vary. Every person selling outbound consulting and every person buying it is looking for that magic script that's just going to blow prospects away. Unfortunately, it doesn't work that way. Your team needs to have the skills to adjust their approach to the person they are engaging.

Trade show negatives

There are a lot of logistics to manage - Most companies will want to hire a full time employee to manage contracts, shipping, booth structure, booth design, and the millions of other things that go into trade show planning.

They are costly - Booth shipping costs are no joke, not to mention the cost of building a booth, securing floor space for it, travel expenses for your staff, and promotional giveaways.

They can get political - Inevitably there will be some political dust-ups around trade shows. Experienced sales reps don't want to spend their time at the booth or don't feel like they should be responsible for sourcing leads for other reps. Marketing fits somewhere in there too: are there other people who should go; how many should you send? We'll touch on these in a later chapter.

Things can (and will) go wrong - Murphy's law definitely applies to trade shows. Something will probably go wrong at just about every show you attend. Recently, we attended a show in Orlando and all of the promotional materials ended up in Miami. Another time we set up a smoothie machine at a booth in San Antonio. It was 90 degrees outside but it was freezing in the convention hall. So while attendees marveled at the idea, the takers were few and far between. The moral of the story is that you can plan, but you can't be prepared for every situation. Something will come up. So it's not about planning for every contingency, it's about building a resilient, capable team that can think on its feet and problem solve.

It's tough to know before you go - One of the biggest challenges you'll face in planning your trade show calendar is figuring out which ones to attend and which ones to leave out. Without on the ground experience, all you have to go by is information from the event host and anecdotes.

So which is it? Inbound or outbound?

As with everything we deal with in marketing, there are no absolutes for every situation. The arguments listed at the beginning of this chapter are largely espoused by people with a vested interest in one strategy or the other (e.g. they have something to sell you).

While it may make for great internet banter, inbound OR outbound is a false dichotomy. Each method has its pros and each method has its cons. It's a mistake to align with one camp or the other while stubbornly refusing to acknowledge their combined effectiveness. It's like saying we're only going to throw one type of pitch because the other one was hit out of the park the last time someone else threw it.

Demand generation is not just about inbound or outbound. It's about getting results. In order to be most effective, we need to put our best performing pieces together and build an approach that adjusts and evolves to meet the conditions we face. In the following chapters we'll dig into the what's and how's of creating high performance inbound and outbound programs that do just that.

Chapter 3

Spring Training |

Laying the

Groundwork for

Success

The aim of marketing is to know and understand
the customer so well the product or service fits
him and sells itself.

Peter Drucker

Aside from, you know, the million dollar contracts, one thing I've always
envied about professional athletes is that each year is precisely mapped out
for them well in advance. They know when the season starts, when it ends,
and even where they'll be on a given date in between. Knowing these items

in advance gives players and coaches the chance to carefully calculate how to use their time. Depending on the time of year, they can spend their time rehabbing to prep for the next game, decompressing after a long season, or preparing for the start of the season.

In marketing and sales, we see at least a poor man's imitation of this as determined by hard fiscal year deadlines and quarterly reports. While we don't have the luxury of a four month offseason, we can take a look at these quarters through the lens of sports and make sure that there's always time for planning, preparation, execution, reflection, and celebration. And if you skimp in one of these areas, the rest will suffer.

The work that you put in during spring training is going to pay off throughout the year. If you are sloppy in training, lazy in setting goals, and careless with your equipment, things will not get better throughout the year, they will get worse, and your team will suffer for it. So take the time to prep, and instead of fixing problems during the season you'll be optimizing for even better performance. Here are a few things to keep in mind when you're preparing:

- Know what you want to achieve
- Provide the information and training to help your team perform
- Maintain your equipment

Know what you want to achieve

We covered this in a previous chapter, but it does bear repeating here. If you don't know where you want to go, you're probably never going to get there. Set your goals using the SMART framework and break them down into manageable (daily, weekly, monthly) pieces so that you can quickly see how you're progressing towards achieving them. I would also encourage you to think about the goal whenever you're planning a new project or even something as simple as a meeting. Starting with the end in mind helps orient everyone towards that goal, and stating it openly keeps everyone together.

Provide the information and training to help your team perform

Again, we talked a little bit about marketing strategy in Chapter 2, but here we're going to dive a bit deeper into the buyer's side of the strategy. I'm sure I'm driving the already-played-out sports analogies into the ground here, but here we're talking about knowing what you're up against. Elite athletes and coaches spend hours reviewing film to identify traits and tendencies of opposing players so that they know how to react when they meet them.

If you truly want to succeed, you're going to need to put the same effort into knowing not only your competition, but also your ideal customer. The good news is that, once the work is done, you have an excellent base to work from and *generally* you're not dealing with 30 other competitors like the pros do. Let's get started.

Building your ideal customer profile

Too often, when bringing an idea to the market we set our sights way too widely. We see the value in our product and assume that everyone else will too. Our first instinct is to share our idea with anyone who will listen. Instead of being laser focused on one niche, we think, "Why would I want to exclude anybody at this point? I'll talk to anyone who wants to talk. The more people I talk to, the more likely I'll be to close a sale. Right?"

In theory, sure, the more people you talk to, the more sales will come through. This is like swinging for the fences every time you're up to bat. Are you going to hit more home runs? Maybe. Are you going to strike out a ton? Bet on it.

Instead of swinging for the fences every time, we do our homework on the pitcher, we stay focused on the pitches we want to hit, we don't chase outside of the strike zone, and we remain patient but aggressively pursue the opportunities we find. By doing this we're going to get to know the niche a lot better and increase the consistency with which we succeed. Perhaps Stephen Covey, author of *The Seven Habits of Highly Effective People*, said it best, "The main thing is to keep the main thing, the main thing."

Identifying the main thing

The idea here is to examine your current client portfolio and look for patterns from the ones you would deem the most ideal. I'm betting you already have some names popping up in your head. Generally, when making this decision we're thinking about profitability, time spent on customer support, renewal rates, etc.

Some questions to ask:

- How many employees does the company have?
- What is their annual revenue?
- Where do they get their funding?
- What industry are they in?
- Who is the end-user?
- Who is the decision-maker/buyer?

- How are decisions made? Is the end-user of your product the decision-maker/buyer?
- How many people were involved in the decision, and how long did it take?
- How did they become a customer? Was it sourced via a trade show, word-of-mouth, your website, or something else?

Using this information, you can begin to build out a profile of what your ideal customer looks like. And with that information you can then begin to figure out where these ideal customers are. From there you determine how to start a conversation with key people at the account, and that gets us to personas.

Developing key personas

The concept of personas really blew up with inbound marketing. And while it has its flaws (people have different personalities, goals, experiences, and challenges which shape their interactions with vendors), in general it's a perfect tool for getting your teams to think about the real live person on the other end of the sales or marketing conversation. Most people will even encourage you to go so far as naming the personas and assigning them pictures. This can be very helpful, and you'll know you've been successful the first time someone throws out the persona name in a meeting.

This is an effective way to bring all of your teams together. Build cross-functional working groups to brainstorm and develop these personas, then share them with the company to refine them. If available, I'd highly recommend getting out of the building and performing qualitative research via conversations with your target personas. We can do a decent job in building a basic persona leveraging our employee experience, but nothing beats the real thing.

In lieu of (or prior to performing) interviews, one place to start is a job description for the key persona. Another secret weapon is checking to see if there are any professional associations for this role. If there are, check out the association's website. Look at what they're talking about and look for conference themes and keynotes. What challenges is the association looking to help its members solve? This often gives you a window into their challenges and motivations.

Here are some key questions to ask when building out your personas:

- At the ideal account, who is involved in the buying process? If more than one person is involved, build out a persona for each.
- What are their challenges?
- What responsibilities do they have?
- How is their performance measured?
- Who measures that performance?
- What are their personal goals? What is the next step up on the ladder for them?
- What makes them look good? What makes them look bad?
- How does your product specifically help address a challenge, make them look good, or help them avoid looking bad?
- To what organizations do they belong?
- With whom do they work on a regular basis?
- To whom do they look for guidance and industry information?
- What blogs do they read? What websites do they visit? Do they still read print magazines? Which ones?
- Where do they get their information?

- Are they more active on one social platform than another?

One thing to note here is that we don't just want to focus on professional traits. Using emotion is one of the best ways to elicit a reaction, so you also want to tap your inner Freud and figure out what these people really want on an emotional level. Most people would probably like to get a promotion, but they probably don't want to get a promotion just to get a bigger paycheck. On an emotional level, they may also enjoy the prestige and recognition that comes with a more senior title.

A final note: this work is important, but it's also important to actually use the information you put together with everything you do. I've seen many companies go through the exercises, pouring hours into honing their ideal customer profile and personas only to disregard it and go right back to the same old MESSaging they've always used when that first email goes out. If you're not going to use the intelligence you've gathered, you're wasting your time and your prospect's time with the same old product-focused pitch they grew tired of 20 years ago.

Instead, put your spring training preparation to work. Tie *everything* back to addressing the concerns of your personas and you'll be well on your way to crafting messaging that resonates with them.

How do we know when the ideal customer profile and key personas are ready?

Part of your job as a marketing and sales leader is determining when good enough, is good enough. You want to be thorough with both your ideal customer profile and key personas, but you also want to move quickly. I've seen companies become hypnotized by the research. They get caught up feeling like they need to spend thousands of hours doing research or thousands of dollars paying a market research firm to get it just right. They end up thinking they are more like psychology professors than marketers.

The key is to do the work, test it, and let the results tell you what to do next. Don't let the perfect be the enemy of the good. What follows are some easy ways to test your personas without risking paralysis through analysis.

If you have a contact who fits the persona profile, maybe a current customer or former colleague, but they don't have time to be directly involved in an interview, ask them if they will do a quick review of your finished product. Ask them if it feels right or if anything seems out of place, or off target.

You may also have someone who holds this position in your own company. Ask them to take a look. Don't forget to reach out to contacts on LinkedIn as well.

Persona development and testing might sound like a waste of time (especially to grizzled veteran sales people), but it's a lot quicker and less painful than trying to go to market with an unclear picture of the market you're targeting. These are powerful documents that can have a huge impact on much more than a single campaign. Put the work in now. The returns will be well worth the effort.

Studying the competition

A SWOT (Strengths, Weaknesses, Opportunities, Threats) analysis is a lightweight way to get your team thinking about your company and where the competition sits in your market.

Grab a conference room and a white board and start brainstorming with your team. To make this productive, you may want to assign competitors to team members ahead of time. Your sales team is a perfect resource for competitive info, and this exercise is the perfect way to share that knowledge with the rest of your team.

You can perform a SWOT analysis on your company where strengths and weaknesses are internally focused and opportunities and threats are externally focused. You can also role play and create a SWOT analysis as if you were working for one of your competitors.

Also, visit websites and trade show booths, and ask your current customers what they think about your competition to stay abreast of what they are doing. I've often had customers who loved our solution forward us marketing materials from other companies. It's a good way to see what is resonating and how the competitors are positioning themselves in the market.

Maintaining your equipment

A final part of your spring training efforts is doing some spring cleaning on your equipment. In this case, we're talking about your database. Data can make or break a campaign. You can have the best messaging in the world, but if you can't get it to the right person it doesn't matter.

After you've identified your ideal accounts and your key personas, it's time to evaluate your database through those lenses. Do you have the right accounts and personas in your database, or is it cluttered with excessive non-niche companies and personas?

Next, is the data accurate? HubSpot estimates that 25 percent of a contact list will expire each year (Miller). Read that again. Each year as people retire, switch jobs, unsubscribe from emails, and change domains, 25 percent of your list will become inaccurate.

This is important for a number of reasons:

Nobody likes spam - If your email's bounce rate is higher than 2-3 percent, you're in danger of being labeled a spammer and that means instead of heading to your prospect's inbox your message is heading to the spam/trash folder. Once you're labeled a spammer it's nearly impossible to get off that list. It's tough enough to get your email read; don't sabotage yourself by sending to expired lists.

Nobody likes wasting time - Time is the most limiting resource we have. If your team is spending its time dealing with bad data, that's less time that can be used for having helpful interactions.

Nobody likes looking like an idiot - Having totally incorrect contact data is one thing, but what if you still get through to that person but their title has changed, the competitive info isn't right, or their name is spelled incorrectly? I'm sure we've all been on the wrong end of a telemarketing call where the caller obliterates our name. What goes through your mind when that happens? I'm not a mind reader, but I bet you're not interested in what they have to say. If our goal is to build trust, all of these things make the prospect lose trust in us before we even get the conversation started.

Clean data is critical and can make or break your operation. Here are a few things you can do to make sure you're staying up to date:

Make a concerted company-wide effort if necessary to validate data - It is that important. You can also have interns or sub-contractors do the grunt work by visiting websites, using LinkedIn, checking Twitter, or calling directly to a switchboard to make mapping calls.

Cross-reference two sources of data - If you're purchasing your data from a provider you can always cross-check what you're getting with other sources of data (e.g., trade show attendee lists).

Hold data vendors accountable - Likewise, if you're paying for data, make sure you're getting what you're paying for. Monitor every wrong contact and report it back to the vendor. If the errors are outside of the accuracy they promise, hold them accountable and/or switch vendors. Don't pay for bad data!

Pre-screen lists - If you aren't sure about the health of your list, you can use email validation services to pre-screen your lists and tell you how healthy they are. This can be invaluable in helping you identify data that needs your attention.

Build your own - Perhaps the best and most efficient way to maintain healthy lists is not to buy data but to build your own opt-in lists via your website and social media. Then every six months or so you can run an opt-in or opt-out campaign to make sure the people on your list still want to receive your emails. This might sound risky, but it's much better than getting dinged with a spam complaint because someone forgot they signed up years ago. Remember, we're focusing on our niche. Quality beats quantity every day of the week.

All right, that's a lot to unpack, but I hope you take it to heart and understand how much preparation can determine performance. Put the effort in early and spend your time improving and optimizing throughout the season instead of fixing and troubleshooting.

Chapter 4

Game On | All-Star

Inbound

> Trust is the glue of life. It's the most essential
> ingredient in effective communication. It's the
> foundational principle that holds all relationships.
> **Stephen Covey**

It's nice to sit down and plan, and if you're following along, we've done quite a bit of that already. But in this chapter we're going to shift from planning to execution. We'll walk through the steps you need to build a high-performing, all-star-worthy inbound program.

What's the difference between all-star inbound and just plain inbound? The difference is that we're going to take the basic tenets of inbound marketing and supercharge them by combining them with some powerful outbound tactics. With this strategy, our inbound all-stars team up with the outbound all-stars to build a dynamic and potent program that improves time to impact, increases audience size, and begins building a database of opt-in fans of your company.

These tactics build trust with each additional interaction and increase the chance that your key personas will reach out to you when they need help. If we do it right, they will even recommend us to their peers before and after they become a customer. Pretty cool, right? Let's get started.

Don't forget your fundamentals

Every great program, product, and team starts with a solid foundation. You can't build anything if the foundation is weak. So let's take a look at the things we need to get right first. We discussed some of this in the last chapter, but we'll put it all together here for easy reference.

Know yourself - What do you want to achieve? Remember, start with the end in sight! Again, this should be a collaborative effort that sets reasonable yet challenging goals.

Know your ideal customer - Who are your best customers, and why did they choose you? Talk with them, review your data, and interview your team to figure this out.

I implore you: If you don't have confidence in the work you've done in these two areas, stop here and iterate until you feel comfortable. Moving forward without a clear understanding of your ideal customer and the key personas of those customers is a waste of time. You'll be creating content that no one cares about and burning through the political capital you've earned to this point. You will need that capital later, so don't waste it by being too eager to get started on *something*. Repeat after me: Activity does not equal results.

The buyer's decision process and mapping the journey

In the last chapter, we prepared for execution by getting to know our key personas better. In this chapter, we're going to focus on outlining the buyer's journey. That is, how do they go about making a purchase, and how do we support them along the way (your company and channel-specific content maps)?

There are a lot of buying/marketing models out there, but I've found a simple three stage outline of the process does the job. It's based on the standby AIDA model popularized by E. St. Elmo Lewis way back in 1898 (ProvenModels). You can get more specific depending on your goals.

Why is this necessary? It will help you create meaningful content and share it at the right time. When we get to creating content, we're going to hold ourselves accountable by mapping each piece of content to a discrete buyer's stage and key persona. We're not just going to say, "Everyone can benefit." That leads to non-specific, non-helpful, and non-impactful content.

Quick Notes

- This is a guide and not prescriptive of every buying situation. Don't be so rigid with it that your buyer's experience suffers.

- As in life, the journey may not be linear; people can bounce from awareness to interest and back several times before moving to the next stage. There's a temptation to draw big black lines between these stages, but it's best to think of these as a more fluid than that. Think about it less like an on/off switch and more like a dimmer switch. This idea will become more important when we start mapping our content to these stages.

The buyer's journey

---

1. Awareness (Problem)

Buyer becomes aware of the product-agnostic problem. Things aren't optimal for some reason or a need is created. The buyer wants to understand the problem better so that they can tackle it.

This is the time to reference your personas. What challenges does your buyer face? When your key customers came on board, what were the issues on the ground that started their search for a solution?

"My car is making a funny noise…"

---

2. Interest (Category-Specific)

Buyer has identified a problem and is researching ways to fix it. Again, this is not product-specific, it is problem-specific. What are ALL of the potential solutions to this problem?

"How much is it going to cost to fix the funny noise?" "How much would it cost to replace the car?" "What is the cost/benefit of repairing vs. buying?"

---

3. Action (Product-Specific)

Buyer has identified the way in which they'd like to solve the problem and is now ready to evaluate the vendors that can help them do it.

"It costs too much to fix the car. I'm going to buy a new one. Which car is right for me?"

Staying aligned

Remember the sample marketing funnel? That looks at the buyer's journey through the company lens. With inbound, though (and especially content), we want to look at it through the buyer's eyes. So to keep everything aligned between our more detailed back-end language and our more simple buyer-facing language, we're just going to map each stage of the marketing funnel to a stage of the buyer's journey.

Just to jog your memory, here's the original one:

Prospect
Buyer has not engaged directly but is on our radar. (Website visitor, trade show attendee, employee at target company, member of target persona professional organization)
Open Lead
Buyer has taken some action to engage with the company. (Website download, webinar attendee, mailing list sign up)
Working Lead
Our team is actively trying to contact the buyer.
Qualifying
Buyer has been contacted by a member of our team and has responded positively but has not been qualified yet.
Marketing Qualified Lead - MQL - Opportunity
Buyer has been contacted by a member of our team and has been declared as qualified by meeting the baseline criteria for an opportunity. An opportunity is created by the person who conducted the qualifying conversation (most likely an SDR). The SDR sets up a hand-off meeting to introduce the contact and the AE.
Sales Qualified Lead - SQL - Opportunity
The hand-off meeting has been conducted. The AE and SDR have debriefed and agreed that the opportunity is valid. The AE will pursue it from here.

And here's a shiny new one all mapped out:

Buyer's Stage	Marketing Status
1. Awareness (Problem)	**Prospect**
Buyer becomes aware of the product-agnostic problem. Things aren't optimal for some reason or a need is created. The buyer wants to understand the problem better so that they can tackle it. This is the time to reference your personas. What challenges does your buyer face? When your key customers came on board, what were the issues on the ground that started their search for a solution? "My car is making a funny noise..."	Contact has not engaged directly but is on our radar. (Website visitor, trade show attendee, employee at target company, member of target persona professional organization)
Exit Criteria	
Contact has taken some positive action to engage with the company.	

Buyer's Stage	Marketing Status
2. Interest (Category-specific)	**Open Lead**
Buyer has identified a problem and is researching ways to fix it. Again, this is not product-specific, it is problem-specific. What are ALL of the potential solutions to this problem? "How much is it going to cost to fix the funny noise?" "How much would it cost to replace the car?" "What is the cost/benefit of repairing vs. buying?"	Contact has taken some action to engage with the company and has been added to a nurturing track. (Website download, webinar attendee, mailing list sign up)
Exit Criteria	
Contact has engaged with the company multiple times and has accrued a lead score meeting a pre-set threshold. Or buyer has reached out for more information.	

Buyer's Stage	Marketing Status
3. Action (Product-specific)	**Working Lead, Qualifying, MQL, SQL**
Buyer has identified the way in which they'd like to solve the problem and is now ready to evaluate the vendors that can help them do it. "It costs too much to fix the car. I'm going to buy a new one. Which car is right for me?"	**Working** Our team is actively trying to contact the buyer.
	Qualifying Contact has been contacted by a member of our team and has responded positively but has not been qualified yet.
	Marketing Qualified Lead - MQL - Opportunity Contact has been contacted by a member of our team and has been declared as qualified by meeting the baseline criteria for an opportunity. An opportunity is created by the person who conducted the qualifying conversation (most likely an SDR). The SDR sets up a hand-off meeting to introduce the contact and the AE.
	Sales Qualified Lead - SQL - Opportunity The hand-off meeting has been conducted. The AE and SDR have debriefed and agreed that the opportunity is valid. The AE will pursue it from here.
Exit Criteria The hand-off meeting has been conducted and an opportunity is being created or the prospect has been disqualified.	

You'll notice there are a lot of marketing stages crammed into the last buyer's stage. That's because on the back end, for us, a lot of things are set in motion when a buyer raises their hand or is qualified. We want to be a lot more detailed on the back end of things so that we can identify issues, but we want to present the buyer with the smoothest, simplest process we can.

I know, it seems like a lot is jammed in there, but it will start to make sense in the next few pages, and once it's done, we don't have to go back to it for a while!

Creating and mapping persona-based content to each stage

Now that we have a general model for how prospects will flow through the marketing funnel, we need to start thinking about how to get them to move through the funnel. That all comes back to the most overused word in marketing in the past 15 years — content. The rise of inbound marketing has led to a deluge of "content" in various forms, some helpful, most not. Unfortunately, many companies and marketers fall into the activity trap. They would rather complete a lot of low quality activities that really only show their supervisors that they were busy and rarely make an impact, instead of a few high quality activities that actually help prospects. That activity obsession has led to mountains of self-centered blog posts, whitepapers, and videos that look really cool but get only 15 views (mainly from the company who published it) the month they're published and are never seen again.

So, how do we avoid this quantity over quality trap?

Be mindful - The first step is just being aware of this tendency. Don't feel like you need to validate your existence or your marketing department by churning out volumes of material. One high quality piece can generate more traffic than hundreds of throw-away pieces.

Focus on your key personas - Remember all that work we put into developing those ideal customer profiles and key personas? Now is when you start leveraging that information. Look back at the challenges and goals that these people face and you're off to a good start in thinking about the types of content they will respond to. Also, don't forget to create content in a format that they are most likely to consume. Busy executives may prefer an easily skimmable article that they can read prior to a meeting versus a five minute video that requires sound.

Get visual - Don't forget to add some visual flair to your posts. Include images, graphics, videos, and other links as appropriate. This will help break up your text and make it easier for today's distracted readers to stay focused.

Think big - Don't fall into the trap of producing one-off pieces that don't fit into a larger concept. Think about a larger concept or challenge and then break it down into several different blog posts or content pieces. Then when you're done, you can combine them all into a bigger piece. Also, don't leave your readers hanging; always include a link to another article, a download, a free trial, something that helps move them toward the next stage in the buyer's journey.

Don't forget keywords - I'm not going to dive into the nitty gritty of SEO here, but too often I see people who fail to make the connection from their keyword lists (generally used for the main marketing site) and their content creation. I know we all think that as soon as we hit publish, the floodgates will open, the content will go *viral*, and the company will soon be planning a parade for the geniuses behind it all. Unfortunately, it doesn't work that way. People will find your content by searching for what interests them, so you need to make sure your content matches what they're searching for.

Here's a questionnaire/checklist that helps hold you accountable:

Objectively, is this persona-centered or product/company-centered?	
Which buyer's stage does it map to? (Awareness, Interest, or Action)	
What keyword(s) are we targeting?	
Which persona does this help? Hint: The answer isn't "All." If it helps more than one, it's probably too broad and won't speak to anyone well enough to motivate them to action.	
How does it help the key persona? What problem/goal identified in our persona work are we addressing?	
Can we reformat it or combine it with other pieces to use it again in a different way?	
Do we have related images ready to go?	
Is it the right format for this persona?	
Is a next step clearly identified for the reader?	

Types of content for each stage

Because the needs of the buyer are different at each stage, we can typically map out the types of content they will find useful relative to the stage they are in.

Quick Tip: The reverse is also true, if a buyer engages with a piece of content that is mapped to a certain buyer's stage, we can infer that they are most likely in that stage.

You can find these diagrams everywhere online, but in general, here's the rundown:

Awareness	Interest	Action
Thought leadership webinar	Solution comparison white paper (Types of solutions - not necessarily products)	Case study
Independent research		Product/feature comparison table
How to blog/video	Case study	Free trial
Tips blog	Industry FAQ	Demo
ebook	Independent product reviews	Customer testimonial
Checklist		
Quiz	Webinar - focused on addressing a challenge (not a full-fledged product demo)	
Evaluation tool (do I have a problem?)		
White paper (describing the problem)		

Also, don't forget that you can start many of these content ideas as several parts of a blog series and then combine them into webinars, ebooks, videos, white papers, etc. So you can start small and build it all or you can build it all and then break it up. Maybe you'd rather build a webinar and then do a blog that discusses the content. Experiment and see what works best for you.

Getting seen

Here are some quick tips for driving engagement with your high-quality, persona-centric (it is high-quality and persona-centric, right?! Just checking!) content.

Boost it - While we'd love to be able to rely only on organic methods of promotion, providing a little boost to your content in the form of advertising is an effective way to get it in front of your target audience. Analyze your organic results on Twitter, Facebook, and your chosen social platforms and then boost the posts that are performing well to see if you can attract a larger audience.

Be consistent - Build out a routine cadence of posts for each piece of content. Don't just do one post and move on to the next. Not everyone is going to see every post you publish. Consistently sharing it out with different messaging and images will help drive sustained engagement.

Leverage your staff - It is getting harder and harder for businesses to organically reach social media users. Provide templates to your staff for sharing out your content via their own social accounts.

Leverage your customers - Share the content with existing customers too if it makes sense. This helps keep them engaged and builds credibility for your content.

Rent some high value space - Contact key publishers and associations in your target industry and find out how you can partner with them to promote your content alongside their in-house work. You can often even work with them to create unique co-branded content which they will publish to their subscribers. This costs money but can be extremely useful as you're building your own opt-in database.

Name drop - I've always thought this is kind of hokey, but lots of people swear by quoting an industry influencer in your content and then letting them know about it with the hopes that they will share it out to their network. I would only do this if it's truly a genuine reference and it adds value that you can't otherwise convey. As with a lot of other tactics, it's been overused and has become less and less impactful.

Viewing the big picture with a channel map

The channel map is essentially your blueprint for success with inbound marketing. Now that we have our content ideas developed and mapped to our key personas, we need to outline how these buyers are going to find and engage with it. That's right, we're literally going to map out how we're going to support potential customers through their buying journey. This is helpful in showing leadership or the rest of the organization what you're up to in marketing.

On the following page is an example of what this could look like. The three stages are listed at the top with related activities falling beneath each. You will note that there are several ways for people to jump into your content. They don't necessarily all start at the first stage (awareness) and work left to right. Depending on where the prospect is in their journey, they can jump in anywhere along the way. Don't just focus on top of funnel awareness offers or you could miss a chance to engage with a motivated buyer.

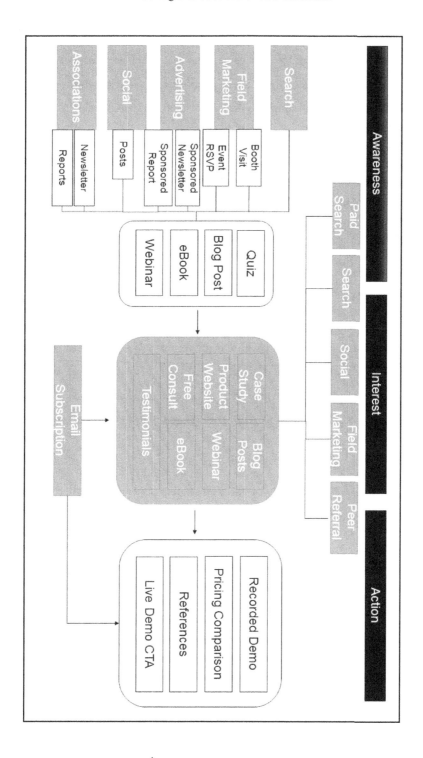

The channel map is a good tool for visualizing the actual steps your buyer will take. Use it to see where you need more content or maybe where you have too much. Typically, companies will do well at generating their top of funnel content (awareness) but fall short in the middle stage (interest) and try to jump straight from awareness to interest. Think of the funnel like a playground slide. If you're at the top with your buyer and you push them off the side, crushing an account executive who was waiting for them to come down the slide, what's going to happen? Even if your AE and your buyer survive that trauma, neither is going to like you very much.

Let's try to avoid traumatizing our co-workers and prospects, shall we?

Moving for the close too quickly will reveal your company as one that's only interested in the bottom line and not truly helping (nurturing) its buyers to be better at their job. It also creates friction between sales and marketing by pushing leads that aren't ready to AEs who are generally pre-programmed (rightfully so) to talk about closing the deal.

Don't throw people off the side of the slide! Your job is to guide them down on their terms responsively, considerately, and professionally.

When you get the journey rolled out, you can start reporting metrics for your content to see what's working and what's not.

Keeping score

A good way to keep an eye on your most active prospects is by assigning scores to every action they take as well as key demographic info like title, company name, etc. You can give them more points for actions that are further along in the buying process to make sure they are quickly visible to your team. For high value actions (e.g., demo requests) you'll want to set up email triggers that notify your team instantly. Overall, though, assigning scores to content interactions gives you the ability to quickly assess who your hottest prospects are and make sure they receive the support they need.

Here's a simple example of some rules you could put in place. Most marketing automation solutions will help you set these up. Some also have predictive lead scoring, but it takes a while for them to gather enough data to be useful. Don't forget to use negative scores for attributes that would lead you to believe it's not a great lead.

Attribute	Score
Website visit	+1
Submitted for for Awareness-stage content	+5
Submitted form for Interest-stage content	+10
Title is one of our target personas	+10
Email is from a free account (Yahoo, Hotmail)	-5

Inbound marketing | 16 mistakes to avoid

1. No research into the content and not targeting it to specific personas.
2. No meat. Content is too thin to warrant a buyer's limited attention. One source articles, no facts to back it up.
3. Not including visuals or no people in the visuals.
4. No keyword research.
5. Product promotion over persona needs.
6. No promotion or no consistent long-term promotion.
7. No master plan. Inconsistent content development and random acts of marketing that don't lead anywhere and leave the buyer wondering what's next.
8. No middle of funnel offers. Handing over unqualified TOFU leads to the sales team.
9. No case studies/proof at MOFU/BOFU.
10. Over the top case studies. Too slanted and clearly biased to have any value at all to prospective buyer.
11. No library on your website. Buyers need an easy way to find resources. They shouldn't have to sort through pages of blog posts to find that one resource they want.
12. Asking for too much info too soon. Overwhelm your buyer with a huge form and they may just run away.
13. Sales and marketing misaligned on strategy and goals.
14. Not repurposing content. One and done.
15. Using "No-Reply" emails. You're building an audience here; give them a chance to speak to you.
16. Overwhelming opt-ins with too many emails. Find the balance between engaging and helpful and overwhelming and needy.

FAQ

How long does it take to start seeing results?

This is one of the toughest questions to answer, but it's something you need to broach with your team. In my experience, inbound takes a lot longer to develop, but in the end the results are much better and more consistent. Before you start developing your strategy, make sure that everyone is on board and aware of the time it will take from the first piece of content to the first qualified opportunity. If you don't do this, the rug will likely get pulled out from your plan before it had a chance to produce real results.

Results also depend on consistency, quality, and visibility (promotional activities) of your efforts. If you're knocking all of those out of the park, you can expect to start seeing impact on TOFU relatively quickly (as soon as you start publishing). You should start seeing qualified leads popping up at around six to eight months and impacting opportunities soon thereafter. Again, results can vary drastically based on the typical sales cycle in your industry and where people are in their journey when they engage with you. So use these numbers as a guideline more than a rule.

If you're plowing through month after month and not seeing any movement, something needs to be re-calibrated; don't wait six months to make a change. Keep focusing on consistency, quality, and visibility, and the results will follow.

6-8 months? Seriously? Can we speed this up?

Inbound is kind of like farming: you need to plant your seeds and let them grow. There's no fool proof way to make the plants grow more quickly. What you can do is give your buyers the opportunity to skip the line so to speak. You can do this by providing visibility to bottom of funnel offers on your site and in your marketing collateral. That way, if a buyer is so inclined, they know exactly what to do. I'm not saying you plaster it in everything you send them; just make it visible in subtle ways. In the next chapter, we'll also discuss what we can do to fill the pipeline while the inbound seeds are growing.

How much content do we need?

At a minimum, start with one piece of content per buyer's stage, per persona, and build from there. As your library of content grows, you can learn from what's popular and create more of that content or even republish it with a fresh update. Don't fall into the quantity over quality trap though!

Chapter 5

Game On | All-Star Outbound

> Many a small thing has been made large by the right
> kind of advertising.
>
> **Mark Twain**

As we noted at the end of the last chapter, one of the biggest challenges with inbound marketing is that it takes a long time to develop consistent results, and there are a lot of ways to mess it up. We're taking a risk by deploying a strategy that takes so long to develop.

One way we can mitigate that risk is by supplementing our inbound strategy with an outbound one. Outbound marketing can help us drive more immediate results and also helps amplify the impact your inbound content can make. This is where all-star outbound differs from traditional sales-oriented outbound: by leveraging our inbound content, we're aiming to put a friendly face on the map for our target customer.

We'll take the sale if it's there, and we may be more inclined to focus on MOFU and BOFU offers, but we're not necessarily trying to close the deal by beating them into submission with call after call.

All-star outbound works in synergy with all-star inbound. We are still leveraging a lot of the work we're doing on the inbound side. We still really need to know our ideal customer profile and the key personas that work there. Using that information we can craft messages that speak directly to the challenges and goals each persona faces. Sound familiar?

There are several types of outreach that fall under the outbound umbrella. We'll go through each, outlining some fundamentals for success and some pitfalls to avoid (i.e., how to do it wrong). A quick note: I tried to include do's and don'ts that were distinct for each tactic, but it should be noted that much of the advice can be applied to others as well, so don't be afraid to apply suggestions across tactics.

Mass marketing
- Advertising
- Mass email
- Direct mail

Field marketing
- Trade shows
- Events at trade shows
- Exclusive dinners
- Open user groups
- Lunch and learn

1:1 sales development
- 1:1 email
- Phone calls

- Social media
- Personal mail

Mass marketing

This one is fairly self-explanatory. Think about it as activities you can do on a massive (1:many) scale.

Common tactics include:
- Advertising
- Mass email
- Direct mail

Advertising

There are many ways to advertise and many people out there who are ready to take your hard-won budget dollars in exchange for advertising. There are old-school print ads, billboards, digital display ads, search engine advertising, boosted social posts, video ads, television advertising, radio advertising, in-app advertising, sponsorships, and the list goes on. In general, I prefer ads that can:
- Be tested and tracked
- Be modified mid-stream
- Help us build our opt-in database of subscribers
- Align our brand with industry thought-leaders and associations
- Supplement our other efforts (inbound content, trade show events, etc.)

The channels and methods you choose will be based on your target market and industry. Below are some fundamentals that are true no matter which platform you choose, along with some common issues to avoid.

Advertising | Fundamentals for success

The 3Rs - Success in advertising is all about the 3Rs - getting the *right* person the *right* message at the *right* time. Run through this checklist as you're putting your strategy and specific ads together.

- Is it targeted to the right persona?
- Is the message/promotion speaking directly to that persona in language they understand?
- Is the message relevant to where they are in the buyer's journey?

Assist, don't interrupt - This is a big change for a lot of old school thinkers and is relevant when we think about all-star outbound marketing. We want to offer a helping hand, not ask for one. We want to add value, not ask for it. So put together assets that will help your personas, not ones that get in the way of your personas accessing the information they are looking for. Be the YouTube video they want to see, not the ad that runs before it. An effective way to do this is partnering with trusted publishers and organizations to create co-branded materials/events that help buyers solve problems. Partnering with trusted advisors helps your brand share that space in your buyer's brain and promotes a positive association rather than the negative one that interruption-based advertising creates.

Keep the conversation going - Just like when you're creating content, your advertising strategy should always have a next step ready to go. And that next step should take them into the appropriate stage of the marketing funnel.

The buyer should never have to wonder what to do next; that's your job. Typically, you'll want to gain their interest by offering something of value. Then you'll want to capture their interest with a form or sign up of some sort. Don't take this as your cue to open the flood gates and shoot them six emails a day for six weeks hoping something will stick. Thank them for signing up, let them know what to expect, and if you think it's appropriate, begin a dialogue with them by asking a question.

Shop around - Don't forget to shop around and compare cost per lead across different providers. Track your own results as opposed to their historical ones. When you have that data in your hand, you have much more power to negotiate better terms.

Five mistakes to avoid in advertising

1. **Assuming the audience already knows who you are and what you do** - This is the classic, product-over-persona fail. You know what your product does, but most people don't. Lead with what they care about.

2. **Entering into an advertising package with a publisher or association without testing** - Don't sign your life away to a vendor you've never worked with before. Many will give you a chance to test out a placement before signing onto a bigger package.

3. **Linking to a generic landing page** - If you're using specific keywords or images to attract your audience, tie the landing page to those same things. If they land on a page that seemingly has no

relation to what they clicked on, they won't stick around.

4. **Not tracking impact** - If you don't have a way to track impact, you won't be able to show the people who are approving your budget where their money is going. As a result, you'll probably get less of it. One of the simplest ways to track impact is by creating specific landing pages for each campaign.

5. **Not following up with content that is relevant to how they converted** - This is another classic one. We want to get started right away, but we don't have any TOFU offers, so let's just offer them a demo! This goes back to working synergistically with the inbound program. Make sure that there's a cohesive next step when someone converts from one of your ads or promotions or you'll risk losing them.

Mass email

Mass email has been much maligned, and people have been trying to kill it off for years. Nonetheless, it has displayed remarkable resiliency and remains one of the most cost-effective ways to reach potential buyers.

Mass email | Fundamentals for success

Opt-in is much better - Build an opt-in list and segment it by persona. The difference between an email sent to an opt-in list versus a cold email is night and day. Think about receiving a phone call from a number you recognize versus one you don't. How much more likely are you to pick up the one you recognize? The same principle applies here (and it will also help them recognize your actual number when you really do call!). Start building your opt-in list as soon as possible, but don't forget to segment it by persona and buyer's stage so that you can send relevant content.

Be consistent and be relevant - Send regularly scheduled, persona-focused content, not product-focused emails. Build workflows that serve up relevant content based on prior engagement.

When opt-in isn't an option, align - If you are just starting out, you may not have a list of opt-in subscribers yet. Align with industry newsletters to sponsor content or place your content alongside theirs. This is safer than purchasing your own list and helps your company avoid the dreaded SPAM tag.

Practice good hygiene - Many organizations will offer you the chance to email their members if you're participating in a conference. This can be a tricky area, but if we're honest, it's also an opportunity to get contact info for people you've identified as important. My absolute number one preference is for organically built, opt-in lists. But, if you are going to purchase data either from a trade show or an industry source, there are a few things to consider.

- **Clean it before you use it.** There are services out there that can help you verify an email list before you send. This will help reduce your bounce rate and potentially keep your deliverability rate up.

- **Check terms and conditions of your email service provider.** Some providers will allow cold emails, some won't. Don't get in trouble with your service provider or get yourself banned for violating their terms of service.

- **Be 1000 percent sure that the content you're offering is going to offer an astounding amount of value to the recipient.** In the case of a trade show, maybe you're looking to invite them to an exclusive dinner. This is much better than, "Hey, check out our awesome product. Click here," leading to your generic home page. I'd also recommend asking a specific question or making it very easy for the recipient to indicate interest (or not). For instance, you can insert links for Yes or No that let someone quickly RSVP for an event.

- **Scale down.** Don't spray and pray. Instead of doing a mass email, perform 1:1 outreach with personalized content.

Limit images - It can be tempting to create an awesome looking, award-worthy, graphic-intense email. An email like that is often immediately flagged as SPAM before it hits the recipient's inbox and is also an instant tell that they are receiving a mass email. Think about it, when is the last time a colleague or friend sent you a personal email that had amazing design elements all over it?

Always be testing - We have the technology, so make sure you're using it. A/B test subject lines to optimize your open rates and then A/B test layouts (colors, CTAs, font sizes, pictures) to optimize for engagement. Don't try to do all of these tests at once; too many variables will make it too hard to determine what's working and what's not. A note on subject lines, though: be truthful about what's in the email; don't employ gimmicks like "re: subject" if you aren't replying to something. You want to establish trust with this person, and lying to or tricking them to get them to open an email isn't the best way to do that.

Four mistakes to avoid with mass email

1. **Blasting everyone the same message** - Remember what we said in the advertising section? Right person, right message, right time. You're going to miss on at least one of those if you aren't segmenting based on persona and buyer's stage. Sending irrelevant emails is the best way to get unsubscribes or SPAM reports.

2. **Adding in tons of media** - I mentioned this above, but it's important enough to mention again. Don't try to shove tons of images and videos into one email. Even if it's perfectly designed, it looks too impersonal and detracts from your core call to action. Pick one call to action and drive it home.

3. **Not considering different devices and platforms** - It's crazy that it happens with today's technology, but I still receive emails that are not optimized for mobile devices. Most email providers will set you up with templates that automatically recognize the device and adjust to make your message fit. Don't forget to check these layouts to make sure they work for every device.

4. **Overloading prospects with emails** - I said in number one that the quickest way to get unsubscribes is irrelevant content. I'd argue that overloading prospects with daily or twice daily emails is right up there as well. My advice is to provide subscribers with options to control the number and frequency of emails they receive from you. If you don't have the expertise to do that, less is always more.

Direct mail

Are we really going to think about direct mail? Absolutely. In the age of phone addiction and screen time concerns, going old school is always something to consider. If you do it right, direct mail can be an effective way to reach executives who are overwhelmed by email or at least to catch the attention of a gatekeeper. And if you earn their attention, they might just be willing to put you through the next time you call or stop by. In fact, according to the Direct Marketing Association's Response Rate Report, response rates to direct mail were actually up in 2017 compared to about fifteen years ago (pre-smartphone). Rates in 2017 were at 5.1 percent compared to 4.4 in 2003 for opt-in lists. For prospect lists the rates were 2.9 and 2.1 for 2017 and 2003, respectively (Conick). Don't be too cool to go old school!

Direct mail | Fundamentals for success

In addition to the fundamentals listed above, here are a few direct-mail specific fundamentals to help you drive results with your next campaign.

Segment by persona - I know, I know, I'm a broken record. Don't forget to segment your content based on who will be receiving it.

Test - We're going analog here, so testing is a lot more legwork, but don't forget to do it. Try to test out different messages on smaller patches before hitting your entire database.

Be unique - Here is where a lot of typical vendors will falter in their direct mail strategy. They send out the same thing that everyone else sends: a bland, product-centric postcard with a less than compelling call to action and some stock photography. If you're going to reach out and do something with direct mail, do it in a way that earns attention. This is an opportunity to stand out and show some personality.

- **Personal** - One of the simplest tactics is to personalize the letter to the recipient. Mention something you read about their company or saw on the news that only applies to them. Or at least throw in a personally signed note with your mail.

- **Lumpy/Dimensional** - Send them something that stands out, literally. A package with a lumpy object in it will at least get some attention, and sometimes that's all you need to open the door to a conversation. I've heard some stories including sending a shovel (willing to do the dirty work), a box of nails (building the future together), and more traditional things like dice (don't roll the dice on your XXXX supplier). The key is to know your persona, and perhaps if you're sending a larger item, really know that person and their personality before you risk offending or aggravating them.

- **Reciprocal** - This is the basis for leveraging your inbound content with outbound campaigns. If you've produced a white paper or a report, you can leverage a hard copy and send it off to them. It has to be of value, though. You can also generate a personalized report for their company and ask for their feedback. The goal is to offer something of value in the hopes that they will reflexively return the favor.

- **PURLs** (Pronounced like *Pearls*) - One way to personalize on a mass level is by creating personalized URLs (PURLs) and placing them on each piece of mail. The PURL can include the prospect's name or some other bit of personalization. This takes some coordination, but it's a neat way to stand out and connect offline methods with online engagement.

Direct mail | Mistakes to avoid

- **Be inauthentic** - If you're going to try to be authentic, be authentic. Don't use fonts that make it look like you signed something if it's truly supposed to be a personal letter.

- **Be disingenuous** - We've all received disingenuous mail, and I'm willing to bet not many of us liked it. Don't stamp things like *open immediately* or *urgent,* on your mail unless it truly is. Again, the goal is to build trust, and tricking someone into opening your mail isn't the best way to do that.

- **Be lazy** - You spent all this time, money, and effort on building your campaign; don't forget to include a next step or set the expectation for your next step. Tell them what to do next or what to expect from you as a next step. The next step can vary based on your goals, but I like telling them to expect a call or visit from the rep. This puts the ball in our court and doesn't ask them to do anything. If you ask them to do something and they don't do it, you're essentially back to square one. If you tell them you will follow up and you do, you are at least a person of your word and are beginning to build credibility with them.

Advertising FAQ

Does advertising still work?

I think most people would say yes to this question, but you can find case studies on both sides of the argument. Some companies brag about never spending a dollar on advertising, and that's awesome. But if your goal is to drive as many qualified opportunities as possible, as quickly as possible, I would recommend at least a small amount of your budget be allocated to advertising. You can always do a small test run, evaluate, and adjust based on the results. Here are a few other thoughts:

- As everyone moves toward digital advertising, it is getting more and more expensive to get results. Direct mail may be a way to stand out from the crowd. Providing a tangible (and valuable) piece of content or a gift takes time, and people inherently understand that. That small realization might just help you get in the door. "OK, she clearly has spent a lot of time on this. I can spare 15 minutes to hear her out."

- Think about advertising in different ways, not just traditional ones. Partnering with publishers on content is a great way to elevate your brand in the eyes of your target audience. Plus, it raises your profile with the publisher which may help increase the likelihood of earning mentions in their editorial content. This isn't suggesting a quid pro quo. I'm just saying that making your brand visible to the editors of the publication simply makes them more aware of it than they otherwise may have been.

- Advertising, combined with your other inbound and outbound activities, creates a multi-channel marketing approach that gives your company the best chance to meet your future customers where they are.

What about Google Adwords?

Adwords is a good choice for people looking to bump up exposure for certain keyword searches, especially if you're struggling to gain organic rankings for them. Be careful, though: you can easily wind up wasting a ton of money if you aren't targeted on the right keywords. Think about fishing with a pole, not fishing with dynamite. And don't fall into the clicks trap. Clicks don't equal conversions. As with any other advertising channel, Adwords needs to be tended to on a regular basis.

How much should we spend?

Start small. Test results, and go from there. Don't spend your entire budget in one shot or with one publisher. You can always spend more if something is working, but you can't retrieve contractually obligated or spent dollars if it's not working.

Field marketing

Field marketing and event marketing can take many shapes. Just like everything else we've talked about so far, it can be done really well if you focus on your key personas, and it can fail miserably if you focus only on your goals. Events are a really effective way to build relationships and trust with your buyers, and they are an essential part of demand generation.

Field marketing activities should:

- Establish trust and rapport between the buyer and your company.
- Create excitement and positive energy around your brand.
- Provide a way for current users to mingle with prospective buyers.
- Help your team quickly identify the buyers from the browsers.

Common field marketing tactics include:

- Trade shows
- Sideshows
- Open user groups
- Lunch and learn

Trade shows - These have been around since medieval Europe, and they probably need no introduction from me. If done well, they can be a powerful asset to your company. If done poorly, they can be the equivalent of hiring Whiplash the Cowboy Monkey as your next CFO: Incredibly amusing, but probably not the best investment for your company dollar.

Trade shows | Fundamentals for success

Know where to go - No matter the company, resources and staff are limited. Trade shows are not cheap, and to do them right takes a lot of planning. Leverage the experience of your sales and marketing team to identify high value shows and weed out the ones that don't make sense. When you are thinking about which ones to attend, ask these questions:

- o Will the right buyers be there?
- o Are enough of the right buyers attending?
- o Is the conference held at the right time, or are there other industry conflicts that may affect attendance?
- o Can we get a good booth location in the show? (Location can make or break a show.)
- o Is there an opportunity to present a session?
- o Are there key industry partners attending? Can we leverage that in some way?
- o Are current customers attending?

Present (if possible) - When you have the shows identified, start researching to see if there is a way you can get one of your customers to present (more about brand ambassadors coming up). No one wants to sit through a boring product demo, so really emphasize the ways in which your customer faced and overcame common challenges.

Plan ahead - Put together a consistent planning process that kicks into gear several weeks/months ahead of each trade show where you outline you pre-show, show, and post-show plans. This should include target personas at the event, communications, staffing, contact info while on site, training, promotions, side events, customer meet-ups, budget, and goals.

- You should also identify whether your account executives will be personally reaching out to drive meetings at the show or whether marketing will handle it all. If account executives will be in attendance, they should be reaching out personally; just make sure the recipient isn't getting two messages from them and marketing.

- As for goals, make sure you know what you want out of the show. Most people want leads, but maybe you just want brand awareness and to get people talking about that booth with the dude in the chimp outfit. Your event strategy should match your goals, so just make sure everything is aligned and working together.

- This is also the perfect opportunity to do a pre-mortem. Instead of waiting until after the event to look at what went well and what didn't, brainstorm ahead of time about what could go wrong. Prompt conversation with questions like, "We didn't hit our lead goal for this show; what went wrong?" and "Our leads didn't convert to opportunities at the rate they should have after this show; why?". This is a useful tool to use across all of your campaigns and can be especially powerful considering the number of things that need to work together for a trade show to be successful.

Giveaways - People like free stuff. It's as simple as that. If your free stuff is good enough, they will trade their contact info for it. While many of these may not be "hot" leads, it's an effective way to build your contact database with target personas. But don't stop there; drive the conversation after the show by offering a second-chance raffle. Tell them to keep their ticket and to visit the URL on the back to register. That URL can tell them a little more about how your company helps people and can help you find out a little more about the prospect. Tadaa - you've got yourself a top of funnel, opt-in prospect!

Create a sideshow - If you can't secure a presentation and/or can't afford a booth presence but you need to be at the show, this is another way to build a presence. Plan an executive roundtable or VIP presentation at a nice local restaurant and invite your prospects. This is not a timeshare, get-them-in-the-room-and-lock-the-doors-style presentation. It's about subtly complimenting your prospect's ego, allowing them to network with others in their field, and providing real value in the form of a guest speaker. The options for these kinds of events are endless. You may have to play with the format to see what works, but these can be a very effective way to open conversations with your prospects. Don't forget to invite current clients!

Put your customers to work - It's one thing to hear a sales pitch from an employee at the booth; it's quite another to hear directly from a happy, paying customer. Brand ambassadors can give an authentic voice to your booth or event presence. Again, you'll want to give them nearly (if not the same) training you give the rest of the booth staff to minimize gaffs, but if you can get them to agree (and you can navigate the legalities) this is a very strong way to improve event performance. As a side benefit, your booth staff gets to hang out and learn more about your key personas, which will help them as they engage with others. Many people will sign up to become a brand ambassador simply because they enjoy your product or service and want to be able to help people learn more about it. But definitely make sure they know you value their contributions. Custom swag, public shout-outs, and *helping* pay for travel expenses are all good ways to show them you care; just be careful not to cross the ethical boundary where the gifts could be seen more like bribes.

Put your partners to work - If industry partners are going to be at the same show, think about teaming up for events, promotions, and prospecting. You can have your staff swing by their booth and vice versa.

This can be powerful if you do it right. Think about it — if you grab a second partner and co-sponsor an event, you've effectively doubled your budget and your reach. Just make sure you choose carefully. Make sure that they truly are complimentary to your service or offering and that you aren't offending other potential partners. You may want to map out a co-sponsorship agreement and strategy with each company rather than building it on the fly. But you (and they) may want to try a pilot event first. In either case, make sure clear expectations are set out, and build in accountability.

Put your team to work - Something will go wrong at every show. Make sure you have the right people on the ground and back home in the office who can problem solve and quickly rectify issues as they arise.

Reward your team - Many companies will set up mini-competitions around lead generation at a show. This can be effective, but often the same person ends up winning over and over. This can lead to other team members simply shutting down. So get creative with the rewards and contests. You get more of what you measure; you get even more of what you measure and reward. Choose creatively and get feedback.

Other field marketing events - Don't forget to try creating your own regional or local events. These can be great opportunities to start conversations with people who are too busy to attend national shows. Make sure you have current customers there, and make sure you're providing something they are interested in. You don't have to get Bill Gates to come to dinner, but you can build a roundtable discussion with current and past executives around a key industry topic.

Train your team - Supply your team with the training and feedback they need to succeed. Help them learn:

- Conversation starters and engaging people as they walk by.
- Your ideal clients and key questions to ask to quickly identify if the person/company is a good fit.
- How to process leads efficiently and with enough context that the team can easily follow up with the right message. Also, train them in how to triage different types of leads. You can do this with the lead scorecard we discussed earlier in the book. If the score is 0-1, it goes to marketing for follow up, 2-3 to sales development, 4 or above to the account executive. You can set it up however you like; just make sure everyone is on the same page.
- How to handle common objections.
- When to hand out giveaways and how many each attendee can have.
- When to provide invites to private functions you may be sponsoring.
- How to handle a live raffle. These can become a little hectic if enough people show up, so some crowd management advice might help the meeker people on your team.
- Booth staffing expectations (number of people, what to wear, etc.).
- How to address competitors when they visit the booth incognito.
- And let's not forget … how to track expenses.

Seven mistakes to avoid with trade shows

Don't train your staff - This seems to be an all too common problem. The company spends all this money on building the perfect booth, dressing it to the nines, securing the perfect space on the floor, promoting a large giveaway, printing new brochures, getting the extra large monitor, and then providing NO training to the staff attending on how to properly engage and qualify a prospect. Granted, the people typically attending shows are salespeople, but there's also a tendency for marketing folks and other team members to show up. No matter how experienced you think your staff are, if you aren't training them, don't complain when they come back with a high expense report and low lead count.

Don't close the loop - Aside from not training the team, this is the second most frustrating thing I've seen happen. Companies put all that effort and money into a trade show and then a) the leads get lost in limbo for six weeks and are never pursued, or, b) no post-event debrief takes place.

If either of these sounds familiar, you're not alone, so don't fret. But by paying careful attention to leads and post-event review, you can dramatically tighten up your team performance, get more of the leads you want, and attend more of the shows you want, while weeding out the ones that aren't effective.

- Outline a clear process for lead triage and build in accountability for follow up. You can set up triggers to notify sales managers if leads aren't pursued within a certain period of time.
- Set up an event debrief a week or so after the event where the team can review final numbers, provide feedback on what went well and what didn't, and discuss/decide what to improve for next time. You

may also want to set up independent feedback sessions to get honest opinions on staff effectiveness. You can also tag a trusted member of the attending staff as the Event Captain, and they can be responsible for individual feedback.

Not knowing your current customers - I'm cringing even as I write this! Make sure that everyone in attendance has reviewed the list of attendees and is well aware of the current customers in attendance. Recognizing them before they identify themselves will get you bonus points. Not recognizing them and treating them like a prospect will not. Do not try to sell your product to someone who already uses it. It won't end well!

Timesharing the audience - By now, we're all familiar with the old bait and switch: Offer something nice and then bolt the doors while you hammer the audience into submission with your sales pitch. We're all familiar with it, no one likes it, but it still happens regularly. If you're doing a special event, dinner, or have even scored a presentation at the show, please, please don't go into a 30 minute demo of your product. No one signed up for it, and no one wants it. Don't imprison your audience; attract them with intelligence, value, and thought leadership and they'll stick around on their own. You'll get to the demo later.

Not offering anything compelling - How many times have you received an email that says, "stop by Booth 429 and say hi!" While I'd really love to one day take that literally and loudly exclaim "HI!" at a vendor booth and then quietly walk away, I don't think that would work out for anyone. Stop by and say, hi? No thanks, I'm good. *delete email*.

Instead, offer a decent reason for them to stop by (food, limited edition shirts, socks, an old screen door, etc. Anything is better than just asking them to stop by to say hello): the SDRs promoting the event and your booth staff will thank you.

I'm kind of joking about the screen door, but think about doing something weird. I've thought way too much about giving away an old 1980s IBM computer at an IT conference. Think about what your personas would find amusing. Instead of competing for the most expensive giveaway, go the other way and compete to be the most interesting. Anything you can do that's out of the ordinary will help grab their attention and snap them out of the email trance.

Mismatching giveaways - Food can be a really effective way to compel people to stop at your booth. Just keep in mind that a lot of these show floors are freezing cold, so be wary of offering frozen yogurt even if you're in Arizona in July. But, you could get creative and offer it outside - after the show, in a banana costume (take it as far as you want!).

Bad booth messaging - If it takes longer than one second for a complete stranger (buyer) to figure out what you do to help them, you should revise your booth design and messaging. Be simple and clear rather than clever. By default, attendees are hardwired to put on the blinders and not make eye contact, so if they do look up, make it easy for them to understand why you're worth their time.

Sideshows - I mentioned this in the trade shows section, but it's important enough to break out here. Sideshows allow you to leverage the traffic and attention created by a trade show to create your own mini-attraction. People are already in town and out of their normal routine; use this to your advantage by creating something of value and building relationships that will benefit you beyond the show itself.

The size and scope of these events will vary based on how important the relationship is and where you are with that relationship. From a marketing/demand generation standpoint, we're looking for small/medium-sized events that can open the door for future conversations. You should rely on your sales team to do the smaller 1:1 style meetings for high priority clients.

Sideshows | Fundamentals for success

Add value - I know, I sound like a broken record, but if you're not doing anything interesting, no one will be interested in what you're doing. Think about what your key personas would want from an event. Free food and drinks are always a good start. But what else can you add that other companies can't or aren't willing to do?

- Can you can leverage your super fans or industry contacts to drive intelligent conversation?
- Is there a hot restaurant in town that you can book way ahead of time?

Make it easy - When you are trying to attract people to an event like this, it is your first shot at showing them how easy it is to do business with you. Don't slip up. Give them the white glove treatment every step of the way. Use personal outreach. Ask if you can register them, don't ask them to register. Follow up with directions, and make sure they know whom to contact with any questions.

Keep your sideshow from turning into a freak show by avoiding these pitfalls

Timesharing - See the note in the trade shows section about this, and don't do it! No one likes to be tricked, and that's definitely not the way to build a relationship.

Overcomplicating things - Make sure that your event is easy to RSVP for and that it's easy to get to. Transportation can be a huge hurdle, so typically the closer to the sanctioned trade show events, the more likely you are to attract people to your event. Also make sure it's clear that the invitation includes space for the prospect to bring some friends.

Bad timing - While you may think your event is the most important thing in the world, your prospects won't. Make sure you cross-check the timing of your event with the trade show and other competitor events. You probably also don't want to schedule anything for the last day of the conference when everyone is heading out of town early.

Open user groups - At my first startup job we used open user groups, and it was one of the most successful ways I've ever found to drive new leads. The idea is to build a showcase around your current users, give them a platform to tell their story, and then let them tell it to their network (which includes people who aren't yet your customers). When done well, this is a win-win-win for you, your current customers, and your prospects. It doesn't get much better than that! These can also be deployed on a local, regional, and national level, so there's no excuse not to give it a shot.

Open user groups | Fundamentals for success

Tell a story that matters - In the startup, we were lucky enough to have hit the sweet spot with our product. The customers we had were die hard fans who were willing to tell their story to anyone who wanted to hear it. They got so much value from our solution that they almost felt it was necessary to share what they were doing with other people. So we let them! We simply provided the platform for them to do it by organizing the event, handling logistics, buying everything, and providing support for their presentation. All we asked in return was that they invite their network of colleagues to the show. By letting them run with the presentation, we allowed them to craft a story that resonated with the target audience and that allowed us to focus more on making sure everything around the event went off without a hitch. Of course, we were there to provide support in crafting the story when needed, but it was very much theirs to tell, not ours.

Let your users take the lead - With other events it can be a little tough to figure out things like the best time of year to host it, the best time of day, the place, etc. By working directly with your users, you can leverage their expertise to take this guesswork out of the equation. Let them tell you the right time and place.

Throw in some additional value - The cherry on top of our user-group sundae with the first company was that one of our executives was actually a very well respected author and thought leader in her own right. So during these local shows, where possible, we'd fly her in to co-present with the user or with our CEO. This enhanced the value people were getting from the user group and added an additional reason for people to show up.

Don't underestimate the power of having an executive show up at events like this. Even if they aren't well known, it can mean a lot to customers and prospects to see that they can get face time with the decision-makers at your company.

Open user groups | Mistakes to avoid

Make it about you - Make no mistake, "you" are not the "u" in user group. This event should be 100 percent focused on end users and making their lives easier. Imagine if you went to a dinner party and the host talked all night long about how amazing he or she is. Now imagine going to a dinner party where the host barely says a word but everyone else is talking about how the host has positively impacted their lives. Which party would make you more likely to want to learn more about the host?

Tell as story that is too thin for your key personas - The value your solution adds to the audience should be unmistakable. One of the challenges I've run into in the past is that we had powerful stories to tell for end users, but those stories didn't resonate enough with the high level decision makers we wanted to show up at these events. While the end user's story may be powerful and very effective in reaching other peers, it may fall flat if the decision-maker is too far removed. Make sure the story you're telling is right for the audience you're telling it to. If you're selling to CFOs, have a CFO tell their story. If the connection is too thin, you're probably better regrouping and waiting for the right user and the right story. Remember, you probably only get one shot at impressing these people; don't waste it.

Don't scope out the environment - This should be a key for any event. Make sure the place you choose is comfortable and adequately reflects your brand. The basement of the local fire hall might be great for the local punk band, but it's not the best option if you're trying to impress the upper echelon of local business. Prospects should walk away wanting to learn more about you, not wanting to take a flea bath (even if Whiplash the Cowboy Monkey makes a guest appearance).

Host a lunch and learn - Did you sigh after reading that lunch and learns are next up on the agenda? Me too. For years, these were a go-to marketing practice that drove leads and promoted conversations. Unfortunately, this practice has been run into the ground by years and years of bad marketing practices, bad *free* lunches, and general wastes of time. It turned more into one-way sales pitches rather than conversations, and prospects started avoiding them. So rather than dive into the ins and outs of this practice, let's just say that if you're going to try it, you better have a really, really, REALLY compelling reason for people to show up. If not, flip the lunch and learn on its head. Use that time to schedule a 1:1 meeting with a current customer to *lunch* and *learn* more about what's going on in their world.

Field marketing FAQ

How many shows should we do?

I would say this is the wrong question to ask. Do your homework and rank the shows you'd like to attend. To make this less subjective, you can score each one on a rubric (key persona, attendee numbers, location, competition, etc.). When you have the absolute musts defined, start with those and work backwards depending on your budget. Then adjust your plans based on your post-event reviews. You'll also have to weigh the pros and cons of attending a large national show versus several regional shows. Often you'll get a bigger bang for the regional buck.

How much should we budget?

This depends on your company and the industry you're pursuing. Trade shows have been big performers for the companies I've worked for, so I wouldn't skimp here, but be diligent and do your homework as well. You can also compare the total cost of a trade show with other activities (content development, SEO, self-hosted events, etc.) to see if attending is going to give you more potential than other investments. Don't forget, you can stretch your budget by partnering with other vendors where it makes sense.

Who should attend?

As long as everyone is getting that baseline training, trade shows are a valuable way to expose different departments and staff to your end users. This can really help them understand why they come to work each day. You can use shows as a reward for those teams who rarely get to leave the office. On the whole though, you obviously want your best account executives there and you want to incentivize them to produce leads even if it's not for their own territory.

If you want to make some noise, see if you can talk the CEO into attending and manning the booth. This can be a neat incentive for people to stop by if they are familiar with your company already.

Lastly, don't forget brand ambassadors. They can really level up the energy and presence at your booth. They're also probably going to tell some colleagues where they'll be.

There are a lot of tactics to choose from; where do we start?

This all depends on your budget, the number of current customers you have, and your goals. I'd recommend trying each of the above tactics a few times each year and figuring out which ones work best for you and your audience. Don't forget to do a post-event analysis so that you can close the loop and improve for next time.

Sales development

Popularized by Aaron Ross's *Predictable Revenue*, the Sales Development Representative (SDR) role has taken off in the past decade or so. If you're building out an SDR team, his book is a must read. I'll also list some other resources in the Further Reading chapter.

An SDR is traditionally assigned to do the dirty work of either simply identifying leads and setting up appointments for the sales team or of identifying AND qualifying leads before passing them off to the sales team.

You will have to figure out what method fits what you're selling, but I prefer having the SDR identify *and* qualify for a few reasons:

- It immediately eliminates the propensity to pass on anything and everything as a lead.
- It drives better alignment between sales and marketing.
- It allows your account executives and SDRs to work more closely together.

- It gives your SDRs a greater sense of autonomy, mastery, and purpose (shout out to Daniel Pink's book, *Drive*). This can help with retention and job satisfaction.

Your SDR program should:

- Establish trust and rapport between the buyer and your company.
- Create excitement and positive energy around your brand.
- Identify and properly route prospects, leads, and opportunities for follow up.
- Provide a semi-predictable revenue stream.
- Help your team build, test, and refine messaging.

We're going to break the fundamentals for success up into two groups. The first one is for managers and provides tips on how to set up the program itself. The second provides guidance for SDRs in terms of best practices for performing outreach.

Sales development managers | Fundamentals for success

Align your people - People often think of SDRs as the missing link between marketing and sales. That leads to a problem: to whom do they report? Sales or marketing? Many companies see SDRs as junior account executives and therefore have them report into the sales team. If that works for you, awesome.

However, I tend to think that seeing them as junior AEs starts them off on the wrong foot, immediately placing them as someone else's subordinate. Morale and engagement play a huge role in whether a rep is successful, so it's important to take every step to make sure they know that they are a valued contributor. Therefore, I like having them report to and be a part of the marketing team.

As I mentioned earlier, this helps close the gap between sales and marketing. By bringing a revenue-centered position into the marketing department, you're orienting the entire team towards it. Suddenly, team meetings aren't just about redesigning a brochure, they're about how that messaging is resonating and how many new leads were generated. This helps everyone begin to connect the dots, and when dots connect, things align.

Does this drive a gap between SDRs and the sales team? Nope! The nature of the work and the way you set up the handoff from SDR to AE naturally drives cooperation and interaction between the teams. That interaction is not inherent in the SDR's work with the marketing team. So, we're forcing more interaction where it doesn't normally exist and letting it happen where it normally does. This also helps drive career development for your SDRs, giving them exposure to two departments instead of one. Pretty cool, right?

Align your expectations - As I mentioned in the opening, you will need to decide whether you want SDRs to generate appointments or to generate qualified opportunities. Whatever you decide, make sure everyone knows what has been decided. Some reps may only want appointments, some may only want opportunities, but it's important to align expectations across the entire process (this includes the rest of the marketing team as well, so make sure they know what you need from them). Also, make sure you clearly and objectively define what an appointment or a qualified opportunity looks like. The less subjective it is, the less likely there will be crossed wires when it is handed off to the AE.

Make the warm handoff - Again, this can vary by your goals, but I'm a big fan of building in a warm handoff from SDR to AE. This means there's a live meeting (typically a conference call) where the SDR introduces the buyer and the AE to each other and provides their understanding of the reason the buyer has agreed to talk with the company. This helps start the relationship off on level ground and allows the buyer to correct the SDR if there were any errors in their summary. After the call, have the SDR and AE debrief to talk about what went well and what didn't, and to document next steps. This will help reduce the likelihood of leads ending up in limbo and helps your team build relationships through these shared experiences.

Side benefit: By participating in these initial discovery calls and hearing the AE take the lead, the SDR is getting free training on how to conduct sales calls and drive prospects further in the sales process. If they ever do want to make the jump to AE, they've already learned some of the basics.

Comparing all these benefits to the only benefit of a cold handoff (time savings) makes it a no-brainer for me.

Give them (some) control - There is a tendency in the industry to treat SDRs like automatons to be programmed with messaging and to perform call after call for eight hours a day, every day. That's why there's so much turnover and burnout within these roles. How much autonomy, mastery, and purpose can you squeeze out of a job where you're given the message to use, the list to contact, and the schedule in which to do it? These types of employees are going to find ways to game the system and will require more and more oversight until finally they burn out and tear down the entire team's morale before quitting or being fired.

Instead of treating them like automatons, treat them like professionals whose opinions matter. Give them training on best practices but invite their input on messaging and allow them to tailor it to their particular style. Work together on messaging, cadences, touch points, and analysis. The more you involve them, the more involved they'll become.

Let them out - Even if they do have input, spending all day every day on the phone and cranking out emails can become monotonous. Your SDRs are supposed to be your top level people at opening conversations and qualifying buyers, so there's no reason you can't deploy them to in-person events as well. This can be a welcome change from day-to-day operations and can also be used as a reward for performance. Letting your SDRs out in the real world will help round out their understanding of key buyers and further develop their rapport-building skills.

Map out their path - Develop a career map that you can share with SDRs which shows them how their career can progress with the company. This shouldn't be a one-size-fits-all approach but instead a multi-branched approach that shows them the skills, milestones, and opportunities waiting for them. This should also include ongoing training, new tools, best practices, and other forms of professional development. These short term and long term rewards can help keep them motivated on days when no one is picking up the phone or responding to emails.

Measure performance with precise account and contact tracking - Set up a consistent process for tracking and analyzing your SDR program. The more consistent you and your reps can be, the more reliable your data will be.

And that will make it much easier to tweak your approach to improve results.

Track:

- The account's status:
  - Open
  - SDR Working
  - Qualifying
  - AE Working
  - Nurturing
  - Not Interested
  - Customer
- The contact's status:
  - Open
  - SDR Working
  - Qualifying
  - MQL
  - SQL
  - AE Working
  - Nurturing
  - Not Interested
  - Customer
- Last interaction (account and contact level)
- Key information
  - Current vendor
  - Adjacent vendors (other technology used relevant to your offering)
  - How to say the contact's name (sounds like —)
- Rep level metrics
  - Activities performed/day/week/month

- o   Activity to opportunity ratio
- o   Opportunities created per week and month
- o   Opportunity source
- o   Messaging responses - what is receiving responses, what isn't? How many touches is it taking to get a response?
- Management level metrics
  - o   Track how many activities are being performed
  - o   Regional metrics - are certain regions performing better than others?
  - o   How contacts are flowing through the funnel
    - At what rate are they converting? How does this compare with industry benchmarks?
  - o   Responses to messaging, positive and negative
  - o   Activities performed/day/week/month
  - o   Activity to opportunity ratio
  - o   Opportunities per week and month

Sales development representatives | Fundamentals for success

Research your contact - If we're honest about it, one of the most dreaded activities a salesperson has to perform is cold outreach. It's uncomfortable reaching out to someone you've never met before and asking for their time. Luckily, cold calling and cold emailing is no longer limited to a name on a list with zero context. Today, we have a ton of resources that can help us craft a tailored message for each contact. The trick today is to make sure you aren't spending too much time researching (avoiding the call) and not enough time calling. Find a balance depending on the importance of the contact and account and also based on the number of contacts you need to reach.

Typically, you can do enough general research in five to ten minutes to build a custom message. Use social media and internet search engines to perform some basic research on your contact and their company.

What are you looking for? First off, make sure that this is the right person and they are at the right company. Often if you're using an internal database your data gets old quickly, so it always helps to verify that they are indeed still at that company and still hold the position you're looking to contact.

Secondly, look for something of interest to them. This can be something as simple as a shared contact on LinkedIn or something more technical tied to a recent press release or earnings call. Just try not to get too creepy or personal. The idea is to show the person on the other end that you see them as more than a name on a sheet and you've done a little homework on how you might be able to help them.
In this way you are already building a relationship by adding value to the conversation rather than asking for it from them.

Next, try to get an idea of where the contact is in the marketing funnel. If the contact came from a trade show or an inbound lead, you have a much better idea of where to start. Check your CRM for past interactions with your company and content. That content should be mapped to specific funnel stages, and that will help you understand what types of things they will find helpful. Then you can work with your marketing team to identify which content will work best. If you can't identify where they are in the funnel, always assume they are higher up. You can always move them down, but if you start with a hard sell, you may never get the chance to move them back up.

You should also pull up your personas here and start trying to tie your messages into the challenges/goals you can help them solve. Better yet, print them out and have them hanging by your desk.

Don't forget to track everything you're learning in your CRM. This will let you quickly pick up where you left off the next time you want to reach out.

Add value with EVERY interaction - Why is cold outreach one of the most dreaded activities? It's because over the years and years of outreach, all the value has been totally removed from these interactions.

Telemarketers and crooked salespeople out for the quick win deployed shady tactics in an effort to get a *Yes*, no matter the cost. Eventually, we all became conditioned to expect the worst every time the phone rings and we don't recognize the number.

Your job is none other than changing that perception from an interaction that extracts value to one that adds it. It's not easy but it can be done, and if you do it right, you'll stand head and shoulders above the others who are after nothing but a quick sale.

You can add value in a number of ways, the first of which is listed above: do your research. Nothing's worse than someone approaching you with a solution to a problem you don't need and persistently trying to convince you otherwise.

When you've completed the research, you can then share items of value that will help them out. This doesn't have to be (and probably shouldn't be) case studies about your company. Right now, you're just trying to get the conversation started based on the research you've done, so everything is about your buyer, not about your product.

If you walk into a car dealer and the salesperson immediately tells you she's got the perfect car for you without asking you a single question, your Spidey Sense is going to go off immediately. But, if she asks you about your current situation, needs, and wants, you're going to feel better about the recommendation she makes. The same holds true for initial conversations with any prospect.

What should you share? Recent press mentions/awards, interesting articles/blogs from respected industry leaders, interactions with other members of the company, etc.

Start small - While we want to add value with every interaction, we also need to resist the urge to throw every relevant piece of information into one email. I'm sure you've received these at one time or another. This is generally a product-centric approach which leaves the buyer wondering two things: "Why do I care?" and "How did this person get my email address?"

Instead of launching into your sales pitch, start with short, punchy messaging designed to simply get a response. One of the more popular ways to do this is to simply ask if the recipient is the right person to answer questions about X. This is tip-toeing on not really adding value, but if you frame it right, it works surprisingly well. It works because it subtly plays to the recipient's ego and also helps them retain control of the conversation. If they don't answer (and you're pleasantly persistent) you're likely going to ask someone else in the company. I've had this happen a few times; if an SDR can't get a response from me, they contact my manager who then requests that I follow up with the SDR. It's much easier to defuse the situation and retain control from the start.

Your goal here is just to get a conversation started. Open that door a crack, then you can build from there. If you start by trying to close them with an 800 word email, they'll probably never answer the door.

Here's an example of what this could look like:

Hi Lisa,

Matt from XYZ consulting here. I work with companies like (ABC reference account), and they've seen improvements in lead gen quantity (up 50 percent YOY) and quality (average deal value is up 25 percent).

Would you be the right person to talk with to see if there's an opportunity to work together here?

And here is a checklist I run through with each message we draft:

- ☐ What we do/Why people work with us
  - ☐ Referral customers, contacts
  - ☐ Mention previous contact, with specific day or date (if applicable)
- ☐ Persona-centric value
- ☐ Call to action (what do we want them to do) or what are we going to do? (They should never wonder about the next step.)
- ☐ Word count < 100-200 words
- ☐ Grammar, spelling

Be authentic - Remember, we're fighting against years and years of conditioning that tells prospects to be very wary of anyone performing cold outreach. The fastest way to confirm that fear is by being subversive or gimmicky. Avoid the lure of short term gains via shady tactics. You're trying to build a relationship here. Build it on solid ground. Resist the urge to try gimmicks like the "re: " subject line or anything that just feels like a trick.

Be consistent - Have a plan in place for how many times you will attempt to reach an individual. Just as you have a plan for driving people through the buyer's journey with inbound marketing, you can also blueprint your outreach to specific contacts. Work with your manager to determine the steps, cadence, messaging, and medium you will use throughout your outreach. According to the *Sales Development Playbook*, most people will stop after one or two attempts to reach a contact. The problem is, according to their same data, it takes at least six attempts to reach at least 50 percent of your leads. You don't need to go overboard and annoy your contact, but you do need to be respectfully tenacious.

Be respectful - I mentioned this above, but it's important enough to mention again. You want to be consistent, but you also need to be respectful of:

- **Their time** - If you do get someone on the phone, make sure that you're prepared. Don't be caught off guard. Practice delivering tight, relevant messaging, and get to the point.

- **Their inbox** - Map out a cadence that is consistent but not overwhelming. You shouldn't be emailing multiple times every day or even one time each day.

- **Their voicemail** - Many reps wonder if leaving a voicemail even matters anymore. I like to advise them to think of it as an audio email but shorter.

This is also an opportunity to show them that you are a professional who has value to add to their day. Be quick, get to the point, and make it easy for them to follow up (by telling them you'll follow up via email). Also, don't think of phone calls, emails, voicemails, in-person visits, and social touches as independent acts. Scope out a plan of attack that deploys all of them in a strategic and well-planned attack.

Sales development | Mistakes to avoid

Don't prepare - One of the biggest challenges for sales development managers can be knowing when to push your SDR out of the nest. I'm a firm believer in a long ramp period with training that covers your product, your process, and your technology. You can do these all at once, but do them! In many cases, SDRs are young professionals being tasked with having conversations with high level executives. Make sure they are prepared, poised, and professional enough to handle the job.

There will be a temptation to just throw them to the wolves and hope that they figure it out. But each bad experience hurts your external prospects and your internal morale. Provide a detailed onboarding roadmap with checkpoints along the way. Include quizzes, role plays, ride-alongs, and whatever else you think can help build a strong foundation. Everything you do will help build confidence, and that confidence WILL be tested every day.

Don't provide ongoing support - As I said above, confidence will be tested on a daily basis. The more your reps feel like they are on their own, the more likely they are to shut down and take it personally. Your job as a manager is to create an energetic, supportive, and fun atmosphere that helps them stay resilient through those tough days. Provide heavy ongoing and predictable support in the form of Q&As, team discussions, and training to keep improving performance and building team confidence.

Don't track anything - In order to become better at anything, we need feedback. For SDRs, feedback comes directly from the prospects, but it can also come in the form of meaningful metrics. So think about the important metrics for your department but also give them access to their own data so that they can see where they may need to improve.

Over-track everything - A surefire way to burn out an SDR and reduce the quality of your output is by hammering them on daily activity numbers each and every day. There is a natural flow to outreach, and overreacting to minor fluctuations will quickly have you labeled as a micro-manager and your team looking for a new job. So keep track of the major metrics, but don't hammer on the little stuff unless you start seeing a consistent pattern of underperformance.

Be creepy - Want to really make sure your prospect never calls you back? Stalk them relentlessly on social media platforms and throw those details into your correspondence. You want to find a happy medium where you can build rapport with someone but not so much that you can recite their biography back to them. Try to find something in common or interesting, and move on.

Sales development tactics

I spoke broadly about how to approach outreach with sales development, but let's quickly dive into each of the tactics along with some do's and don'ts. Note - there are tons of resources out there on specific scripts to use, so we're not going to rehash that here, but definitely take some time to dig through them, try them out, and see what works for you. Just remember that everything has a shelf life; your messaging should be constantly evolving and improving based on the specific feedback you are (or aren't) receiving.

Common sales development tactics:
- 1:1 email
- Phone calls
- Social media
- Personal mail

1:1 Email | Fundamentals for success

Always be tracking - Everything you do from an outbound perspective should be done with an eye on how it can be tracked and analyzed. Sales development is an art and a science, and modern tools can help you track, analyze, and improve your results, but only if you're tracking them.

Always be testing - As the saying goes, if you can't measure it, you can't manage it. Once you've got the tracking in place, you can start testing different approaches. Side note: make sure you're giving your messaging, subject lines, and other variables enough time to work. Sending ten emails and switching everything out doesn't give you a statistically significant basis from which to make decisions. I recommend sending at least 50 emails before switching out a variable.

Things to test:

- Subject line
- Opening line
- Call to action
- Signature
- Title used in signature
- Send times
- Titles you're sending to

Keep it simple - It can be tempting to throw everything but the kitchen sink into one email in the hopes that something will catch your prospect's attention. Unfortunately, this has the opposite effect: too many details blind them to the one thing that might matter to them. Keep it simple and keep in mind that this is one point of contact in a series; you don't need to throw everything you've got in one shot. Think of it like a pitcher setting the batter up for a strikeout. You can't strike them out with one pitch; you need at least three.

Email | Mistakes to avoid

Testing too much at once - While we always want to be testing and it can be tempting to test everything, that's not how testing works. Small things like font size and colors can have major impacts, let alone major changes like copy and subject lines. Make sure you're only testing one variable at a time so that the results can provide you with information to move your outreach forward.

Giving up too soon - This is a fine line and you'll have to learn how to walk it depending on your industry and persona's characteristics. But you definitely want to make sure you are making enough attempts to get through to the prospect. This doesn't mean being annoying. As long as you're adding (real) value with each send, you're being pleasantly persistent, not annoying. If you feel like you're being annoying, go back and look at how you can tweak the message so that you're assisting, not interrupting.

Treating email as the Holy Grail - It's really easy to think of email as the only outreach tool you need, but it's also lazy and ineffective. Think of email as one tool in a multi-faceted approach to starting a conversation rather than the only thing to use.

Phone calls | Fundamentals for success

Practice, practice, practice - Even all-stars take batting practice, and everyone on your team can benefit from practicing phone calls. Grab anyone and everyone you can to role play with you before getting on the live call. You'll be surprised how quickly it goes from feeling lame to helping you craft a crisp, confident message.

Explore improvisation - Scripts are nice. They give you some training wheels when you are learning to ride, but you need to be able to make the script your own. I encourage reps to take a basic message but to play with the wording so that it feels natural and conversational. Some of the best Hollywood moments have come when actors were allowed to go off-script and do what felt right for the moment. Nobody wants to be on the sending or receiving end of a 100 percent scripted conversation.

Be human - All too often, reps go into outbound mode where they just want to hammer through as many calls as possible so they can get back to checking email and social media. This also happens with prospects. They recognize it's a sales call and immediately shut down and depersonalize the call. Slow down, take a breath, and empathize with the people you're reaching out to. Listen to how they sound, and respond in kind. Build rapport by mentioning something you have in common or read about in your pre-call research. Do something to snap them back to reality and to help them realize that you're both humans trying to do a good job.

Visualize it - Know where you want the call to go before you pick up the phone. You can even take a play from pro athletes and envision how the call should go. I know it sounds hokey, but give it a try.

Look at the tape - With email you can (and should) be going back to look at the key metrics affecting your performance. With phone calls, you can look at quantity numbers, but there's a lot of qualitative stuff within each call that can't really be boiled down to a metric. Take the time after each call or calling session to think about what went well, what didn't, and what you'll do to improve for the next one.

Phone calls | Mistakes to avoid

Quitting too soon - Cold calling is hard, and it's even harder when someone tells you no. The initial reaction is going to be to take the easy way out, say thank you, and move on. While we don't want to be annoying, we do want to make sure we've provided the prospect with enough information to make sure what we're offering is not of value to them. So you need to be a little persistent, and often times you can open up a conversation on the second or third attempt. Try to bat down at least one objection before giving up.

Not preparing - This can range from not knowing who you're calling to not knowing enough about the industry or your products to hold a decent conversation. Nothing comes off as more of a waste of time than someone who doesn't know who they are talking to or what they are talking about. Put the time in to know your product and your personas before calling, and your confidence will shine through in every call.

Social media | Fundamentals for success

Become a resource - Your social media presence isn't about sharing every press release your company puts out. It's about setting yourself up to be a trusted resource for quality information. Try to share relevant articles (from your company and others) every day, comment on other feeds, ask questions, and give compliments. We all know that negative emotions tend to resonate on social media, but that's not the best tactic here. Stay positive.

Be consistent - If you're going to establish a presence, make sure you stick with it. If you have a three year old Twitter account that hasn't been touched and still has the egg profile picture, you're not really helping anyone.

Be selective - Social media is always evolving, and it can be tempting to try to have a presence on each and every platform. For me, it's better to pick the ones your personas are active on and go deep on those particular platforms rather than broad on all of them. It's easier to manage. Let your marketing team worry about all the up and coming platforms and whether they are right for your company's efforts.

Social media | Mistakes to avoid

Be a blabbermouth - We've all had run-ins with those accounts that just can't seem to shut up. They are the reason the mute button was invented. Be consistent but don't be overwhelming. Once a day is plenty for a broadcast post. Go for quality over quantity; most platforms will reward you for posts that receive interactions and punish you for mass posts that don't receive any traction, so focus on that.

Be unprofessional - Be careful with the language you use and the images you share. Everything is a reflection of your personal brand, and your company and the landscape is littered with people who've had the power of social media backfire on them for an off-the-cuff post.

Break the dinner party rule - Social media is like a huge party that everyone in the world is attending. It's a good idea to abide by the old rule of thumb and avoid discussing religion and politics on your professional feed. Chances are it's not going to end the way you wanted it to.

Bonus tactic: Snail mail

Before we wrap up the sales development piece, I want to quickly mention a tactic that's still effective and somewhat underutilized in today's digital world - the personal, handwritten letter.

A well-crafted handwritten letter shows that you've taken the time to think about the recipient and conveys a personal touch that's tough to duplicate. I like to layer snail mail into outreach campaigns as one more way to catch someone's attention. All of the above do's and don'ts apply, and obviously it's tough to scale, but give it a reasonable shot and see what happens. If nothing else, it gives you a good reason to follow up with a call or email.

Sales development FAQ

What is the best AE:SDR ratio?

3:1 is a fairly standard ratio, but it all depends on your budget. One is better than none, but stretching your SDR staff too thin will, at a minimum, hamper your ability to quickly identify what's working and what's not.

How many calls/emails/activities should an SDR be doing to be successful?

Check out the Benchmarks chapter later in the book for the research I've been able to compile on this subject.

Cold/warm calling, really?

Yep, but maybe not for the reason you think. It's more about establishing your company in the contact's mind and showing a degree of professionalism. Anybody can batch email 1,000 contacts. By taking the time to call and leave a message, you're showing a level of engagement that others aren't willing to offer. Honestly, if you are too embarrassed to call someone and offer them help, you may need to revisit your value proposition. If you genuinely feel that your company can help them and are genuinely interested in helping them, it only makes sense that you would reach out to offer your support.

Chapter 6

Building Your All-Star Team

People are not your most important asset.

The right people are.

Jim Collins

Through the first few chapters of this book, we've explored a good bit around inbound and outbound marketing and why it's so powerful to use them together. But a strategy is only as good as the people implementing it. To run this baseball analogy into the ground some more, if we're building a team and we hire the best left fielders we can find and ONLY left fielders, we're not going to get the best results. Instead, we outline the positions where we need players to play based on our strategy and then build the team based on the skills needed for each position.

This is a very important chapter. I've seen way too many hours wasted with too many left fielders. If you're building your team from the ground up or you've already fielded one, you need to stay laser focused on making sure the team you have matches the performance you want to achieve. So make sure your team is crystal clear on individual, team, and departmental responsibilities and build a culture where it's OK to ask if something is in a gray area.

Of course, the blueprint laid out here is one of many varieties that you can deploy, but I like this model because it has a relatively small footprint and it helps drive alignment between the sales and marketing departments.

We'll start with the three Cs of team building for demand generation, the three Ps of training, and then dive into the positional framework.

The three Cs

Cooperation - Avoid lead limbo by ensuring there are no gaps in lead coverage. One of the biggest and most impactful mistakes companies make is generating leads and then letting them fall into lead limbo. Marketing thinks sales is following up, sales thinks marketing is following up, and the lead is left floating in the ether until they get mad and go somewhere else. You've done all the hard work to generate this lead; this should be the easy part!

As you're setting up your team and running campaigns, define which position is responsible for following up on which leads. This should be as unambiguous as possible, and every sales and marketing team member should have a crystal clear understanding of the process. This helps keep everybody accountable.

Communication - Keep SDRs and marketing in the loop on sales developments - pipeline, big wins, big losses, etc.

- Allow SDRs to join sales meetings as well. It will give them the same ability to draw a line from what they're developing to sales opportunities.

....

The SDR secret weapon

Advocate that the sales development rep work directly with the marketing team. This achieves two things:

- It bridges the revenue gap between sales/marketing. It also helps the marketing team draw a line from the campaigns they are running to the leads and opportunities that are being developed.
- It elevates the position on the marketing team instead of making it grunt work for the sales team. This also provides different exposure to elements of the company, different career paths, not simply a one-way ticket to AE status.

Compensation - Reward your entire marketing team for qualified opportunities. This helps orient EVERYONE towards the end goal and reduces the likelihood that they will hide behind vanity metrics (followers, page views) and the ever-nebulous "brand awareness." Focus them instead on conversion rates, cost per lead, funnel development (moving from one stage to the next), MQLs, SQLs, Opps, and closed won.

- It doesn't have to be a lot. Variable compensation is not typically a part of marketing work, so even the smallest commission or bonus can help drive the behavior you're looking to achieve.

- Goal setting and compensation - Determine a base rate for each measurable achievement, and build it based on encouraging the results you'd like to see.

- You get more of what you measure. Define the metrics that they will be compensated for, and provide a window for them to check their progress.

The three Ps

As you build out the framework for your team, you also need to think about how you will prepare them to deliver all-star caliber support for prospects and customers. You can hire the most gifted people in the world, but if you aren't training them on the people you're selling to, the product you're selling, and the process your company follows, it's going to be a rocky road.

As part of your onboarding program, build out separate certifications that help them develop a basic understanding of these three areas. I like to mix up the onboarding so that they gain exposure to each area a little bit at a time; you don't need to have them focus all on people before moving on to product and process. This helps keep things interesting and reduces the information overload that so often overwhelms new hires.

People - This training is all about learning the key personas to which your company markets. Your key personas will help a great deal here but nothing replaces in-person interactions. Make it a goal to introduce new hires to a few key personas within the first few weeks.

Product - This training is all about learning the ins and outs of your product. I once worked with a startup that gave the same onboarding training to their new employees as they did new customers. It was a wonderful way to download a bunch of information and develop a uniform knowledge base across the company.

Process - This training is all about the technology and specific processes your teams use to get the job done. This can be anything from marketing automation and CRM training to hand-off procedures.

Putting time and effort into these key areas will go a long way towards helping your new hires succeed. They immediately feel like you've invested in them and begin building confidence right out of the gate. It also allows you to establish a baseline of accountability.

Don't forget to check for understanding and to continually improve the onboarding process based on feedback and real-world results.

The All-Star Team Framework

Marketing Roles

Marketing Team Lead

Description: This position serves as the hub for all things demand generation. Traditionally, this person would be your marketing manager. This role differs in that it requires hands-on execution rather than straight management. Eventually, the position could grow into a leadership role but it's important to have this person executing on the ground floor. It provides them with great experience and lets them build a career based on real accountability. Unlike a hands-off manager, they can't hide behind performance issues of other staff members. Once they prove they can run these initiatives well, they will be better off in training someone to take over the day to day and also better equipped to manage that person.

Responsibilities:

- Orients the team to lead generation
- Brings strategic vision to tactical operations
- Conceptualizes and executes lead generation and development campaigns
- Lead ownership: Makes sure the right leads get to the right person at the right time
- Builds cooperation and alignment across the team and departments (sales/marketing)
- Develops KPIs and process for capturing related data
- Provides coaching and development opportunities for the rest of team
- Manages budget
- Owns recruiting
- Fills gaps in team as necessary
- Keeps executive team abreast of campaign performance, bottlenecks, and team morale
- Is responsible for delivering a set number of qualified leads and marketing opportunities.

Reports to:

- VP of Sales and Marketing

Key Traits:

- Broad skill set to provide management and coaching across the team
- Digital advertising, social media, marketing automation, budgeting
- Creative
- Experimentally minded

Compensation:
- Base salary
- Variable compensation based on:
  - Qualified opportunities created by the team
  - Individual goals achieved
  - Team goals achieved
  - Sales goals achieved

Field Marketing Representative

Description: This person is responsible for all of the company's in-person event marketing. They work closely with both the sales team and the marketing team lead to plan and execute any variety of the events we described in chapter five. We carve out this role simply because there are so many logistical considerations that it's best to have one person solely dedicated to handling them.

Responsibilities:
- Event research
  - Costs, dates, deadlines
- Event oversight
  - What events are we going to?
  - Metrics management and tracking
    - Lead ownership - Making sure the right leads get to the right place at the right time.
  - Pre-post show communications
- Logistics management
  - Who is going?
  - What is going?

Reports to: Marketing Team Lead

Key Skills/Traits:

- Attention to detail. Must have! Ask anyone who has ever ended up in Tampa for a trade show when their booth and collateral ended up in Orlando.
- Creativity
- Outgoing
- Willingness to travel
- Exceptional budgeting and tracking abilities

Compensation:

- Base salary
- Variable compensation based on:
  - Qualified opportunities sourced
  - Closed won sourced
  - Individual/Event level goals achieved
  - Team goals achieved
  - Sales goals achieved

Sales Development Representative

Description: This person is responsible performing 1:1 outreach to prospective buyers.

Responsibilities:

- 1:1 outreach to targeted accounts
- Account/contact research
- Crafting and testing messaging
- Tracking results

- Following up on *qualified* leads

Reports to: Marketing Team Lead (Not the sales team. See the Outbound section for more information on why we do this.)

Key Traits:
- Patience
- Tenacity
- Positivity
- Some computer skills or ability to learn
- Attention to detail
- Target industry knowledge a big plus

Compensation:
- Base salary
- Variable compensation based on:
    - Qualified opportunities sourced
    - Closed-won sourced
    - Individual goals achieved
    - Team goals achieved
    - Sales goals achieved

Sales Roles

Team Lead/Sales Director

Description: This is the traditional sales leadership role, responsible for hiring, coaching, managing, and potentially selling as well. This person serves as the sales peer to the Marketing Team Lead. The two work closely together to ensure proper alignment across the departments. This role also works closely with the Field Marketing Representative to plan events.

Together these roles are responsible for bringing in and closing your deals. Choose wisely!

(*We set this up as a peer relationship to encourage teamwork rather than a master/servant style dynamic where the marketing team feels it has to do whatever sales tells it to do. Ultimately, these sales and marketing roles will report into a VP of Sales and Marketing, CEO, or another executive depending on the size of your company.)

Responsibilities:
- Sales hiring
- Sales coaching
- Sales process development
- Executive briefings
- Budgeting
- Event attendance and staffing decisions
- Key account meetings
- Pipeline tracking and reporting
- Coordinating with marketing on lead generation initiatives and lead follow ups
- Coordinating with Customer Success on new client accounts and handoffs

Reports to: VP of Sales and Marketing

Key Traits:
- Self-starter
- Positivity
- Direct communicator
- Successful sales experience AND successful coaching experience

Account Executive

Description: This is the person responsible for qualifying opportunities and closing deals. These people are critical in the demand generation program, taking the qualified opportunities marketing develops and closing that business, turning them into satisfied customers.

Responsibilities:
- Account prospecting and development
- Qualifying and closing sales
- Attending sales and marketing events
- Developing customer relationships for success stories
- Following up on qualified opportunities
- Territory planning (with Field Marketing and Marketing Team Lead)

Reports to: Team Lead/Sales Director

Key Traits:
- Self-starter
- Positivity
- Direct communicator

Sales Enablement (Operations) Manager

Description: This person is responsible for helping everything run smoothly on the CRM side of the house. They provide reporting support, develop best practices, and set the tone for what should and should not happen in your CRM.

Responsibilities:

- Help AEs make better use of CRM
- Work with SDR(s) to streamline data input
- Provide insights from CRM data
- Act as the data police
- Set up alerts and notifications for key activities
- Help with reporting and analysis
- Provide support and organization for related collateral
- Analyze and optimize sales processes to remove bottlenecks and improve efficiency

Reports to: Team Lead/Sales Director

Key Traits:

- Data and process-driven
- Technically oriented
- Highly organized
- Sales experience

Customer Success Roles

Account Manager

Description: This person is responsible for nothing less than making customers' dreams come true. Marketing has helped customers identify the need, sales has proven that your solution (above any others) can help, customer success delivers on that promise.

Responsibilities:

- Strategic planning with customer
- Onboarding (bringing the customer up to speed)

- Ensuring the transition from prospect to customer is smooth
- Providing customer support
- Answering day-to-day support questions

Reports to: Sales Director

Key Traits:
- Self-starter
- Proactive
- Target industry experience
- Problem-solver

Additional Roles

If you have the capacity to add more staff or are ready to add more firepower to your program, here are some good places to start. Depending on the skill set of the person you hire, these roles would either initially be handled directly by the Marketing Team Lead or outsourced by them.

Marketing Communications Rep
Responsibilities:
- Mass email marketing
- Marketing automation
- Advertising research and planning
- Website, landing page management

Design Resource
Responsibilities:
- Design support for all marketing activities
- Trade show banners, brochures, giveaways

- Website graphics
- Email marketing

Interns

Short on cash? Don't discount the power of an intern. If you have the time to set up the program, it can be beneficial for you and the intern, giving them valuable experience in a real-world setting and potentially developing a new talent pipeline for your team.

Just beware, while interns can be a huge benefit to your team's productivity when oriented the right way, they can be the exact opposite when they are not. Instead of helping increase productivity, they take away time from you and other team members because they are never sure what to do. Take the time to build out the program with explicit goals, tasks, and deliverables and provide ongoing monitoring and feedback (more in the beginning) to make sure they are on the right track. Then, when they're ready, give them some more responsibility. Interns are kind of like puppies: they can bring energy and enthusiasm to the environment, but they do need to be managed closely. Keep that in mind and it's a win-win for everyone involved.

Hiring the right people

We opened up this chapter with a quote from Jim Collins: "People are not your most important asset. The right people are." As we round out this chapter, it's important to circle back to that quote to drive the point home. You can have the perfect framework, the best strategy, and a great product, but if you don't have the right people, you are going to struggle.

I've included some traits as well as key skills needed for the positions we've outlined, and these are good starting points. To hire the right people, though, you will need to go deeper to make sure you're building the right team for your company culture. This is all about finding the right fit for the way you and the company at large operate; what intangibles are going to complement those that are already in-house? Ask questions that get to the heart of these traits during the interview process.

Take your time in hiring, and don't be afraid to be creative. Ask prospective team members to provide sample work or do things to get to know the real person, not just the best-face-forward interviewee. I know one team of hiring managers that plays smart cop, aloof cop, to try to see how prospects respond to each. This helps them understand how these folks might respond when interacting with people like this on a day-to-day basis.

This is also an opportune time to revisit the intern discussion. Internships can be a great way to determine if there's a potential long-term fit for both parties. And at the very least, you can figure out what you don't want for a particular role.

Your demand generation programs always need to be evolving and improving with each iteration, and so does your team.

That leads me to one of the tougher recommendations in this book: If you make a mistake with a campaign, you address it, learn from it, and move forward. The same can be said for talent management. Take all the steps you can to help build their confidence in themselves, the company, and their craft. But don't blindly keep charging forward with weak staff members who refuse to learn, change, or adapt.

You aren't doing ineffective staff members any real favors by letting them know they can stay gainfully employed with poor work ethic, and they certainly aren't helping you. One bad attitude can drag down an entire team; don't let it drag yours down! I'm not saying you need to be a ruthless dictator. I'm all about giving people the feedback and the tools to improve; it's when they refuse to try that you need to act.

Check out *Radical Candor* by Kim Scott for some ideas on giving meaningful feedback.

I'll leave you with another quote, this time from David Ogilvy:

> *Hire people who are better than you are, then leave them to get on with it. Look for people who will aim for the remarkable, who will not settle for the routine.*

Chapter 7

Working Inbound and

Outbound Together

Being busy does not always mean real work.
The object of all work is production or
accomplishment and to either of these ends there
must be forethought, system, planning, intelligence,
and honest purpose, as well as perspiration.
Seeming to do is not doing.
Thomas Edison

We've covered a lot of ground in the first chapters, haven't we? By now,
we've established what the all-star demand generation strategy looks like,
the pros and cons of inbound and outbound, the fundamentals for success

with each and traps to avoid. We've also covered how to structure your team to drive maximum alignment and results.

By now you're probably thinking it's time to press "Send" on some campaigns, publish some pages, and get to work. Frankly, if you've made it this far without thinking that, I'm impressed. But if you remember, my favorite saying is, "Don't confuse activity with results." Just doing something isn't better than waiting to get it right. Remember, you'll likely only have one (maybe two) shots at impressing a prospect. Make sure it's with your best one.

Using the all-star strategy involves a lot of moving parts. Right now, before you hit *Send* or *Publish*, is where a little extra work can save you from plenty of headaches in the long run. Here are a few additional considerations we need to cover before we launch.

Set your goals - This is basic but bears repeating. Set SMART goals for the sales and marketing department all the way down to the individual and campaign level. Make projections based on what you know, and adjust them based on the results you see. On the campaign level make sure you are defining what success looks like before you launch. Remember, campaigns don't necessarily have to end in close-won opportunities; a campaign goal could be to increase top of funnel leads by a percentage or hard number or to get X number of people registered for an event.

Set your goals, including what success looks like; make sure everyone is on the same page. If everyone starts on the same page, they are a lot more likely to end on (or at least near!) the same one, but if you never try, some people may not be reading the same book!

Keep your data straight - Data, data everywhere and not a drop that's useful. How many CRM systems have you worked with that were either a) filled with old data that couldn't be trusted, b) filled with bad data that was never right, or c) filled with data so unorganized that only one person in the whole company knows how to glean anything useful from it? Again, we're often victims of our own desires to get going on something because we fail to set up repeatable processes that add value (rather than destroy it) with each action. Data is so important to every enterprise. That's why I encourage you to have someone on staff who is responsible for CRM optimization and sales enablement.

Build a system that gives you a clear window into your data, and it will repay you in kind. Priorities should include developing a system that clearly defines who owns which accounts, tracks recent interactions (inbound or outbound), and alerts the account owner to key events. The easier it is to use and the more value your team sees from it, the more likely they are to use it.

Set the schedule - Inbound and outbound campaigns can run at the same time, but they shouldn't be hammering the same people at the same time or you'll wear out your welcome before you get started. Think about how much space there should be between an outbound calling campaign and an outbound marketing campaign, and also make sure you're adjusting your messaging based on whether the prospect has interacted with any of your inbound assets.

Build an account team - Again, there are a lot of moving parts when you're running inbound and outbound campaigns side-by-side. Without careful consideration and properly maintained CRM outlined above, it can be very easy to cross your wires. That can mean two reps contacting the same prospect, a prospect not having their question answered, or even current customers receiving marketing promotions.

One way to avoid crossing wires is setting up your CRM the right way; the next failsafe is building account teams. Account teams let your sales development and sales executives pair up on prospecting territories. Because they are working together on a regular, rather than happenstance basis, they inherently begin to know what's happening at each account. This builds alignment and a level of trust that helps them work more closely together. This can help avoid slip ups in prospecting, but don't forget to train them to check the account for ANY activity before performing outreach.

Perform a pre-mortem - It's fairly standard practice (at least it's fairly standard recommended practice - whether it's actually done is another story) to perform post-mortem reviews of marketing campaigns and projects in general. This is an effective way to take a look at how a campaign performed, learn what went well and what didn't, and improve results for next time. This should be a part of every demand generation program.

What's not so standard (*yet,* anyway) is a pre-mortem. Instead of waiting until after the campaign is published and the wheels have fallen off, pull everyone into a room and brainstorm what might go wrong before you launch. Then devise ways to make sure these things can't happen. This is an awesome idea that can help you head off major mistakes as well as minor but impactful ones.

Having said that, **don't be afraid to make mistakes.** Be afraid of making them and not learning anything. Microsoft CEO Satya Nadella said it best in his book *Hit Refresh*:

> *We need to be willing to lean into uncertainty, to take risks, and to move quickly when we make mistakes, recognizing failure happens along the way to mastery. Sometimes it feels like a bird learning to fly. You flap around for a while, and then you run around. Learning to fly is not pretty but flying is.*

And lastly…

Don't confuse activity with results! Busy doesn't always equal better.

> *It's not enough to be busy; so are the ants.*
> *The question is: what are we busy about?*
>
> - Henry David Thoreau

Chapter 8

Creating Lifelong Fans with Customer Success

We asked ourselves what we wanted this company to

stand for. We didn't want to just sell shoes.

I wasn't even into shoes - but I was passionate about

customer service.

Tony Hsieh

This wouldn't be a true demand generation book without at least a mention of one of the most important aspects of generating demand, your current customers. In fact, it's probably worthy of its own book. For way too long, sales and marketing teams focused on closing the deal, high-fiving, and moving on to the next deal without putting much thought into whether the new client is receiving what they were hoping to from the product/service they were sold.

This chilly handoff inevitably leads to misaligned expectations, overworked customer success teams, and if you're in software-as-a-service, a to-do list for the programmers three years long based on promises one overeager sales rep made to the prospect to close the deal. Anybody can tell you that's not a sustainable way to run a business or help people. And if you're not helping people, you're not going to be in business very long.

Instead of treating the closed sale like the end of the road for sales and marketing, we should think of it like a loop. Closed customers shouldn't fall off the radar; they should become brand ambassadors that can supercharge your marketing efforts through trade shows, events, sideshows, testimonials, user reviews, and webinars. A peer's endorsement means so much more than generalized marketing speak from a paid company representative. User reviews are becoming more and more important as consumers look to cut through the noise and find the truth. In fact, according to the Spiegel Research Center, displaying five or more user reviews can increase conversions as much as 270 percent.

The good news is, you can use your marketing automation and CRM systems to help automate the onboarding process and lighten the load for your customer success team. Automated onboarding emails can show new customers the ropes, share commonly used resources, and help them build steam as they grow into your service. You can also set up automated notifications to let your team know when certain milestones (positive and negative) are hit.

By automating the rote tasks, you free your team up to provide more personalized service on the more complex use cases. Your onboarding process will vary depending on the product/service you provide. In general, if it is a complicated and expensive offering, the process should be hands-on, punctuated with live interactions, and measured in milestones. If it's less complicated and less expensive, you can think about relying more on automated, self-serve options.

Don't forget to encourage your team to be proactive about engaging with clients or to establish a working understanding of how often and when they will be reaching out. It's also a good idea to establish goals (SMART ones, of course!) with clients and put project plans in place to hit those goals. Then when it comes time to review/renew contracts, your team can point to all the progress you've made or point to areas where progress wasn't made with ideas on how to fix the shortfalls.

Remember, if your team isn't calling your customers, you can rest assured that someone else's team is. You've deployed a lot of effort and resources to bring these customers in the door; don't let them slip away now. Set goals, hold everyone accountable, and get after it!

Chapter 9

Tools & Technology

Technology is nothing. What's important is that you have a faith in people, that they're basically good and smart, and if you give them tools, they'll do wonderful things with them.

Steve Jobs

OK, there's a reason this is one of the last chapters in the book. It's so that you put most of your initial planning into what you want to accomplish and how you want to do it.

Software can be a monumental time saver, but it can also be a monumental time waster if we use it as a way to cover up a lack of strategy or a lack of faith in the people you hire.

Having said all that, there are some amazing tools out there, and they are getting smarter every day. Here are a few of my favorites, industry standbys, and some recommendations from colleagues. Placement in this section is not meant as an endorsement; I just wanted to share a few names to get you started in finding the right tools for your situation.

Project tracking - You can make this as complex or as simple as you like. I prefer lightweight solutions that are easy to manipulate and share across teams without having to create logins for everyone, so I've fallen back on Google Sheets and Excel on more than one occasion.

- Asana
- Basecamp
- Google Sheets
- Microsoft Excel

Marketing automation - Pretty much a necessity for a full-fledged demand generation program. These can do a lot of the heavy lifting that would otherwise have to be done manually.

- HubSpot
- InfusionSoft
- Mailchimp
- Pardot

Email marketing - Perfect for getting started and building lists at a much lower cost than full-on marketing automation platforms.

- AWeber
- Mailchimp

- Vertical Response

1:1 Email (SDRs, AEs) - This is where I do see technology providing a big benefit over manually tracking campaigns. Reps can get notifications when prospects open or click emails and can also get metrics that help them/your marketing team craft better messages.

- Close.io
- HubSpot Sales Pro
- Outreach
- PersistIQ

CRM - This is typically the mothership when it comes to your company's data, but make sure you know what you want to get out of it before making your purchase. You don't necessarily need a Ferrari to drive to the post office.

- HubSpot CRM
- Microsoft Dynamics
- Salesforce
- Sugar CRM

Chapter 10
Further Reading

There are worse crimes than burning books.
One of them is not reading them.

Ray Bradbury

Looking to get more in depth about specific topics or explore related topics? Here are some recommendations for further reading (in no particular order).

Marketing

- *Purple Cow: Transform Your Business by Being Remarkable* by Seth Godin (and anything else he writes)
- *Influence: Science and Practice* by Robert Cialdini
- *Crossing the Chasm* by Geoffrey Moore
- The *Modern Marketer's Field Guide* by Matt Heinz

- *Made to Stick: Why Some Ideas Survive and Others Die* by Chip and Dan Heath
- *Gravitational Marketing: The Science Of Attracting Customers* by Jimmy Vee and Travis Miller
- *Word of Mouth Marketing* by Andy Sernovitz
- *Blue Ocean Strategy* by W. Chan Kim and Renée Mauborgne

Management

- *Radical Candor* by Kim Scott
- *The SPEED of Trust: The One Thing that Changes Everything* by Stephen M.R. Covey
- *Drive: The Surprising Truth About What Motivates Us* by Daniel H. Pink

Sales Development

- *The Sales Development Playbook: Build Repeatable Pipeline and Accelerate Growth with Inside Sales* by Trish Bertuzzi
- *Predictable Prospecting: How to Radically Increase Your B2B Sales Pipeline* by Mary Lou Tyler and Jeremy Donovan
- *Predictable Revenue: Turn Your Business Into A Sales Machine With The $100 Million Best Practices Of Salesforce.com* by Aaron Ross

Chapter 11

Benchmarks

The All-Star Game was one of my top highlights
as a player. In my eye, it gave me a good idea
of where I ranked among my peers.
That was always my benchmark to say that I am
still in the upper echelon of players.

Scottie Pippen

Just like baseball (or basketball) stats can help you tell who is an All-Star
and who is not, benchmarks can help give you an idea of how your team is
doing. However, use these with caution. Every industry and situation is
different. Check for updated stats when possible as these numbers are
always moving. And please check out the people and companies whose
work is cited.

Goals

- Average monthly SQL total using BANT qualification: 9.6 per month (TOPO)
- Total activities
  - 125 per day (49 dials, 75 emails, seven conversations) (TOPO)
  - 140 per day (50 calls, 65 emails, 20 social/personal) in seven hours (Sweat)
- Pipeline created
  - 49 percent of revenue sourced by SDRs (Bertuzzi)
  - Pipeline contribution from prospecting: 40-60 percent (InsightSquared)
- Conversion rate
  - Eight per qualifying conversation (PersistIQ)
  - Two percent of prospects contacted (Sweat)
- Pass rate (How many conversations turn into appointments for sales?): 60 percent (PersistIQ)

Calls

- Minimum calls to contact at least 50 percent of leads: 6 (Bertuzzi)
- Most reps give up between one and two attempts (Bertuzzi)
- Dials per day
  - 60 (Top performers 200+) (InsightSquared)
  - 50 average (Sweat)
- Dials per connect
  - 10 (InsightSquared)
  - 12 (Tyler and Donovan)

- Dials per qualifying conversation: 30:1 (Tyler and Donovan)
- Dials per appointment: 90:1 (Tyler and Donovan)
- Connects to appointments: 12 percent (InsightSquared)
- Dials to opportunity: 150 (InsightSquared)
- Cost per appointment: $700 (InsightSquared)

Cold Emails

- Email open rate
  - 35 percent (Close.io);
  - 45-60 percent (PersistIQ)
- Response rate (positive, negative, neutral): 10-15 percent (PersistIQ)
- How many to send per day
  - 40-100 (Close.io)
  - 65 (Sweat)

Chapter 12

Common Terms

Our business is infested with idiots who try to impress
by using pretentious jargon.

David Ogilvy

Ogilvy wasn't one to mince words, was he? Marketing is filled with jargon
and acronyms that can make simple conversations sound like a physics
exam. It's best to try to avoid using jargon. But even if you don't use it,
other people will. Here are a few common terms that are bound to pop up
when you are talking about marketing and demand generation.

A/B test - This is shorthand for comparing two versions of something and
running an experiment to see how each performs. You'll typically see this
when discussing landing pages or Google Adwords ad versions.

AE - This stands for account executive. A traditional salesperson who is
responsible for generating and closing new business.

BANT - Qualification method which measures the prospect's budget, authority, need, and timeline for purchase.

BOFU - This stands for bottom of (marketing) funnel. Prospect knows a lot about your brand/solution and is actively considering purchasing it or a competitor's.

Conversion rate - The rate at which prospects perform the call to action on a specific page. If 100 people visit a page and five of them sign up for an offer, the conversion rate is five percent.

CTA - This stands for call to action. The action you want the prospect to perform after seeing your messaging.

CRM - This stands for customer relationship management. In most cases, we're talking about the software that helps you manage and track the sales process as well as customer data.

KPI - This stands for key performance indicators. Metrics developed to analyze program or staff performance.

Marketing funnel - The process that a prospect goes through in order to become a qualified lead and make a purchase. It's called a funnel because you will have more people at the top than at the bottom.

MOFU - This stands for middle of (marketing) funnel. Prospect knows more about your brand/solution and is actively engaged with your marketing.

MQL - This stands for marketing qualified lead. The definition will vary by company.

Pipeline - This refers to the amount of business a company expects to deliver over a certain time period.

PURLs - This stands for personalized universal resource locators. Web addresses that are customized to the recipient. Typically, including their name, company, or something similar.. It is pronounced like *pearls*.

SaaS - This stands for software-as-a-service. Many popular companies offer software-as-a-service (Salesforce and Spotify are two good examples).

SDR - This stands for sales development representative. A front line staff member responsible for prospecting and building brand awareness.

SEO - This stands for search engine optimization. It refers to the process of developing or editing page content that will increase the likelihood of ranking highly for specific keyword searches done with search engines. You will often hear the term *organic rankings* when discussing SEO; these are the rankings and positions on a search results page that you can't pay for. The spots must be earned with optimized content.

SEM - This stands for search engine marketing. Instead of organically ranking your page with search engine optimization, the spot on the search results page is paid for through an advertising agreement with the search engine.

SMART goals - This is one of the most enduring and widely adopted acronyms I've run into. It was first used in a 1981 issue of *Management*

Review in an article called, "There's a S.M.A.R.T. way to write management's goals and objectives" by George T. Doran. In his version the letters mean: Specific, Measurable, Assignable, Realistic, and Time-related. However, in the most commonly used version the letters stand for Specific, Measurable, Achievable, Relevant, and Time-bound.

SQL - This stands for sales qualified lead. The actual definition will vary by company.

TOFU - Sorry, we're not talking about delightful vegetarian dishes. This stands for top of (marketing) funnel. Typically when the prospect is just getting to know your brand.

YOY - This stands for year-over-year. It is typically used when comparing one month to the same month in prior year.

Chapter 13

90 Day Demand Generation Plan

One of the best mental disciplines for people
to implement is simply putting together a schedule
or a task list and actually executing it. Write the list
or the schedule the night before, and then do what
you said you would do. Life becomes much better
when you do that.

Jocko Willink

This chapter provides an outline of the activities and outputs needed to get
your demand generation program ready for business. The plan includes
three stages which provide you with the opportunity to review existing
operations and performance, apply that knowledge in developing a strategy
for moving forward, and learn from initial campaigns to continuously
improve your results. I hope you find it helpful as you look to put the

lessons from this book into practice. I've listed related chapters below each stage.

Please note that while stage one is fairly standard, specific deliverables in stage two and three will vary based on your current situation and capabilities. Accordingly, please use this as a guide rather than a specific blueprint. Set SMART goals for your project, and remember this is just the first 90 days; you will be able to come back and polish up other items as you develop the program.

Stage One | Analyzing Your Existing Audience and Operations
(~30 days)
Introduction and Chapters 1, 2, 11

Stage Two | Optimizing Operations and Building Your Audience
(~30-60 days)
Chapters 3, 4, 5, and 9

Stage Three | Long Term Audience Development and Demand Generation
(~60-90+ days)
Chapters 6, 7, 8, 11

Stage One | Analyzing Your Existing Audience and Operations

(First 30 days)

In stage one, we take an empathetic look at our target audience and a dispassionate look at our operations to discover who our best customers are and what we need to do to find more of them.

There are two main projects in this phase:
- Know the audience
- Know yourself

Know the audience

Build a profile of the ideal customer so that we can speak their language and offer value on their terms. Who are our best customers and why? How did we acquire them? How can we replicate the acquisition process? How can we find more ideal customers? And where do they hang out online and in person?

Know yourself

Examine channels, process, and technology through the lens of lead generation. Determine what's working and what's not. Identify areas for improvement in current state, define desired future state, and provide tactical recommendations to bridge the gap. Review revenue goals and establish metrics. Identify additional resources needed.

Analyze existing and past pipelines. Determine where to focus engagement efforts. Are we getting enough leads but not converting them? Are we not getting enough leads? Are people responding to outreach at all? This will determine how to focus our lead generation efforts in stage two (top of funnel, mid-funnel, bottom of funnel, or the entire funnel).

Key deliverables in stage one

Ideal customer profile - Conduct research and analysis to determine the company's high value customers and create a profile for future prospecting. The goal is to define a market segment (or segments) that are distinct enough to target and large enough to provide adequate opportunities for demand generation.

Potential segments:
- Firmographic
- Operational
- Situational

Target persona(s) - Conduct research and analysis to determine key personas involved in the purchasing process; define their key challenges, decision-making process, and key influencers.

- One page profile per identified target persona
- Influence map charting key decision-maker, direct influencers, and indirect influencers

Operational summary and demand generation action plan - This report analyzes your organization's current state and puts together a plan to bridge the gap from where you are to where you want to be.

It includes:
- Overall analysis and recommended path forward

- Current state by channel
- Recommended future state by channel
- Tactical recommendations
- Additional resources needed to complete recommendations
- Estimated goal numbers (Contacts, Leads, Opps, Closed)

Lead process review - This project involves reviewing lead management and providing recommendations for improvement if needed. At the end of the project we will have clearly defined marketing lead stages and the criteria for handing a lead off to an account executive.

Lead scoring rubric and scorecard - Developed in collaboration with the sales team, this resource provides a quick way for your teams to evaluate and triage leads. It also helps establish the common language needed to help improve sales and marketing alignment.

Stage Two | Optimizing Operations and Building Your Audience

(30-60 days)

In stage two, we take what we've learned in stage one and begin operationalizing that knowledge to engage and attract the target audience.

Projects in this phase include:
- Evaluating and optimizing technology
- Event research and planning
- Outbound campaigns
- Creating content for the target audience
- Promoting content

Evaluating and optimizing technology - Using the lead process review and channel assessment from stage one, analyze how information is currently flowing into the marketing automation, CRM, and related systems and make modifications. The goal is to automate what we can and optimize what we can't.

Event research and planning - Determine relevant, upcoming trade shows or events and develop cohesive action plan for marketing around them.

Outbound campaigns - Determine target audience and develop multi-touch integrated promotional campaign(s) designed to drive more immediate results and build brand awareness.

Creating content for the target audience - Using the knowledge from stage one, create content which addresses challenges, misconceptions, and other issues for the target audience. Map that content to each stage of the funnel and the buyer's journey.

Promoting content - Begin engaging target audience by deploying social, email, and digital advertising to promote lead magnet and blog assets.

Key deliverables in stage two

Event guide - This template serves as your team's resource for planning and executing field marketing events. They will fill it out prior to each event.

It includes pre-event planning, an event plan, a post-event plan, and a post-event review.

Pre-event plan

- Promotional items
- Giveaways, raffles
- Second chance raffle (post-show)
- Target personas
- Adjacent events
- Staffing
- Communication plan
  - Pre-event 1:1 email(s)
  - Pre-event phone call(s)
  - Pre-event mass email
  - Advertising

Event plan

- Scorecard for quick lead assessment and triage
- Giveaways, raffles

Post-event plan

- Triaging leads for prompt follow up
- Follow up plan for hot, warm, and cold leads

Post-event review

- Contacts made (raffles, promotions, non-purchase intent leads)
- Leads generated (qualifying conversation took place, threshold met)
- Status of leads (followed up, untouched, etc.)
- Opportunities generated
- Lessons learned (stop, start, keep doing)

Campaign guide - This template serves as your team's resource for planning and executing integrated campaigns.

It includes:

- Target personas
- Target location
- Target industries
- Call to action
- Timing
- Goal response rate
- Associated messaging and visual workflow
    - Email 1 copy and subject line
    - Email 2 copy and subject line
    - Direct mail copy
    - 5-7 point SDR follow up cadence and messaging
- Post-campaign review
    - Email metrics vs. industry standards
    - Response rate vs. expected
    - Leads generated
    - Opportunities generated
    - Lessons learned (stop, start, keep doing)

Advertising opportunities and associated partnerships menu - This worksheet serves as your team's resource for research related to advertising and association sponsorship opportunities.

It includes:

- Related associations or publishers
- Audience reach
- Relevant persona/industry
- Cost
- Relevant dates
- Contact info for the association or publisher

Content calendar - This worksheet plans and tracks content creation with content mapped to concepts, keywords, targeted persona, and stage of buyer's journey.

Content publishing - After the content calendar is created, it is time to start creating and publishing content.

- Create several calls to action on blog.
- A/B test to optimize for engagement.
- Compile blogs into ebook.
  - Create landing page.
  - Draft landing page copy.
    - Two sets for A/B testing
  - Create contact form.
  - Publish ebook landing page.
- Draft social posts to promote content.
  - Twitter
  - Linkedin
  - Facebook
  - Other platforms as defined in stage one
  - Related images
- Boost high performing posts with advertising.

Website updates - Begin optimizing the web site to become a lead generation machine. Update home page and product page content based on keywords and personas.

- Apply recommendations from stage one analysis.
- Build and launch search engine marketing campaigns.
- Perform link building outreach.

- Remove friction for conversions.

Technology optimization - Begin working to tie your related systems closely together. Decide what data gets pushed and/or pulled to which system, and begin reporting on that data.

- Develop a dashboard for tracking KPIs and activity.
- Automate notification emails for key events.
- Optimize lead flow from various channels.
- Integrate between systems where possible.

Stage Three | Long Term Audience Development and Demand Generation

(60-90+ days)

In stage three we leverage the work we've done in the first few stages by deploying additional content to nurture leads, conducting more outbound campaigns, analyzing results, and modifying our approach to improve results.

Projects in the phase include:
- Lead nurturing and development
- Additional outbound campaigns
- Analysis and continuous improvement

Lead nurturing - Build trust by nurturing subscribers with relevant content (based on lead intelligence). Inch them toward SQL threshold or buying intent activities (pricing page, demo request, consult). These activities would start as soon as prospect converts so it could happen earlier than the final 30 days. It depends on how quickly you can ramp your content creation.

Additional outbound campaigns and events - Continue conducting outbound campaigns and attending events, but remember to analyze results and put plans in place to improve each time.

Analysis and continuous improvement - Analyze metrics to determine what's working, what's not, and where you can use more horsepower.

Key deliverables in stage three

Lead development workflows by persona - For this project we map out how we are going to try to guide a prospect from one stage of their journey to the next.

- Email copy
- Email design
- Segmentation and configuration
- Lead scoring

Monthly newsletter - This is a good way to resurface blog content and highlight areas of expertise.

Continued blog and content development mapped to key personas - Content development will be constant, but remember to focus on quality, not quantity.

Marketing calendar - Now that things are up and starting to move, it's a good idea to put your plans into some kind of tracking resource. Review results from stage two campaigns and develop a marketing calendar for the following 30-60 days.

- Identify effective tactics.
- Deploy additional resources to support effective tactics.
- Modify ineffective ones.
- Experiment with new ones.
- Leverage the advertising and partnership menu from stage two and deploy targeted campaigns to promote content created in stage two.

90 day review - Think of this as a mini version of the operational audit from stage one. What is our current state, and what do we need to do to improve from here?

- Leverage dashboard from stage two to analyze performance.
- Perform team surveys and feedback sessions on persona and ICP effectiveness.
- Depending on your sales cycle, new customers may be coming in.
  - Ensure they are the right fit.
  - Review onboarding program.
- Review these reports:
  - Marketing funnel analysis - How many contacts, leads, MQLs, SQLs, are we getting and how quickly are they moving through the funnel?
  - Campaign influence report - How are our campaigns impacting opportunities?
  - Channel analysis - Leads by source, Opps by source, Conversion rate by source.
  - Opt-in contact growth

Thank you for reading!

For related articles and resources, please visit

www.demandgenconsulting.com

Works Cited

Bertuzzi, Trish. *The Sales Development Playbook: Build Repeatable Pipeline and Accelerate Growth with inside Sales.* Moore-Lake, 2016.

Close.io. "Cold Email Hacks." *Close.io Resources*, 2017. https://resources.close.io/coldemailhacks. Accessed 25 Jan. 2019.

Conick, Hal. "How to Use Direct Mail in the Modern Marketing Mix." AMA, Aug. 2018, www.ama.org/publications/MarketingNews/Pages/how-use-direct-mail-modern-marketing-mix.aspx. Accessed 12 May 2018.

InsightSquared. "The Definitive Guide to Building a Successful Outbound Lead Generation Team." *InsightSquared Resources*, 2014. https://www.insightsquared.com/wp-content/uploads/downloads/2014/05/ebook_prospecting_v6.pdf. Accessed 19 Sept. 2018.

Miller, Melissa. *The Email Campaign You Need to Clean Your List & Re-Engage Subscribers.* https://blog.hubspot.com/blog/tabid/6307/bid/33403/the-email-campaign-you-need-to-clean-your-list-re-engage-subscribers.aspx. Accessed 31 Aug. 2018.

PersistIQ. "How to Choose, Track and Improve Key Sales Development Metrics for Predictable Growth." *PersistIQ Blog*, 2016. http://blog.persistiq.com/how-to-choose-track-and-improve-key-sales-development-metrics-for-predictable-growth. Accessed 18 Aug. 2018.

Pink, Daniel H. *Drive: The Surprising Truth About What Motivates Us.* Penguin, 2011.

ProvenModels. "AIDA Sales Funnel - Elias St. Elmo Lewis." https://www.provenmodels.com/547/aida-sales-funnel/elias-st.-elmo-lewis. Accessed 31 Aug. 2018.

Ross, Aaron, and Marylou Tyler. *Predictable Revenue: Turn Your Business Into a Sales Machine with the $100 Million Best Practices of Salesforce.com.* Pebblestorm, 2011.

Schultz, Mike. "Is Relationship Building in Sales Dead?" *RAIN Group*, 24 June 2014. https://www.rainsalestraining.com/blog/is-relationship-building-in-sales-dead. Accessed 18 Aug. 2018.

Sweat, Julianne. "How Many Meetings Should a Kickass SDR Schedule Per Month?" https://www.linkedin.com/pulse/how-many-meetings-should-kickass-sdr-schedule-per-month-sweat. Accessed 31 Aug. 2018.

TOPO. "The 2016 TOPO Sales Development Benchmark Report." *TOPO Blog,* 2016. https://blog.topohq.com/emergence-strategic-sales-development-2016-topo-sales-development-benchmark-report. Accessed 25 Jan. 2019.

Tyler, Marylou, and Jeremey Donovan. *Predictable Prospecting: How to Radically Increase Your B2B Sales Pipeline.* McGraw-Hill, 2016.

Made in the USA
Coppell, TX
12 August 2022

81385355R00098